# Discover

## BRIAN ABBS · INGRID FREEBAIRN

*STUDENTS' BOOK 1*

Longman

# Contents

| LANGUAGE USE | LANGUAGE |
|---|---|
| **LESSON 28 I'm doing my homework.** | |
| Ask and say what you are doing | What are you doing?<br>I'm doing my homework.<br>Are you writing a postcard?<br>Yes, I am./No, I'm not.<br>You're writing a letter. |
| **LESSON 29 She's wearing Number 13.** | |
| Ask and say what people are doing | What is he/are they doing?<br>She's/They're running.<br>She isn't/They aren't diving. |
| Talk about order | They're second.<br>He's last. |
| **LESSON 30 Roundup** | |
| **LESSON 31 Do you like hamburgers?** | |
| Ask and talk about likes and dislikes | Do you like hamburgers?<br>Yes, I do./No, I don't. |
| Say what people like | Maria likes chips.<br>She doesn't like milk. |
| Talk about tastes | I don't like onions.<br>I don't like mustard, either. |
| Ask for food in a restaurant | Can I have some chips, please? |
| **LESSON 32 Which ones do you like?** | |
| Ask about and identify things you like | Which bag do you like?<br>I like the pink one/that one.<br>Which shorts do you like?<br>I like the red ones/those.<br>Do you like that sweater/these/those sweaters?<br>Which one/ones? |
| Agree and disagree with people's tastes | Yes, I like it/them too. |
| Express approval | It's/They're really nice. |
| Offer assistance | Can I help you? |
| Refuse assistance in a shop politely | No, thanks. We're just looking. |

| LANGUAGE USE | LANGUAGE |
|---|---|
| **LESSON 33 When have we got Maths?** | |
| Ask and talk about your school timetable | When have we got Maths?<br>On Monday.<br>We've got Science on Friday afternoon. |
| Ask and talk about your best subjects | What are your best subjects?<br>My best subjects are maths and science. |
| Exclaim | How horrible! |
| **LESSON 34 Do you like swimming?** | |
| Ask and talk about likes and dislikes | Do you like swimming?<br>Yes, I do./No, I don't.<br>I like playing tennis.<br>I don't like swimming. |
| Compare likes and dislikes | So do I.<br>Neither do I. |
| Compare skills | So can I.<br>Neither can I. |
| Talk about people's likes and dislikes | George likes swimming but he doesn't like playing tennis. |
| **LESSON 35 Roundup** | |
| **LESSON 36 A big golden Labrador.** | |
| Ask about and describe animals | What's special about a giraffe?<br>What's it like?<br>It's got a long neck and large spots. It lives in Africa. |
| **LESSON 37 It's too high!** | |
| Ask and say what the matter is | What's the matter?<br>It's too high! |
| Complain | Our school day is too long. |
| Give orders | Let go and drop! |
| **LESSON 38 Speak loudly and clearly!** | |
| Criticise the way people do things | You're speaking too quietly. |
| Instruct people to do things in a certain way | Speak loudly and clearly.<br>Shut the door quietly. |

| LANGUAGE USE | LANGUAGE |
|---|---|

## LESSON 39 How tall is it?

| | |
|---|---|
| Ask and talk about measurement: | |
| height | How tall/high is it? |
| | It's 83.03 metres tall/high. |
| | How tall are you? |
| | I'm 1.55 metres tall. |
| length | How long is it? |
| | It's 260 metres long |
| width | How wide is it? |
| | It's 29 centimetres wide. |
| depth | How deep is it? |
| | It's 7 metres deep. |
| distance | How far is it from London to New York? |
| | Its 5,565 kilometres. |

## LESSON 40 Roundup

## LESSON 41 How much are they?

| | |
|---|---|
| Ask and say the price of articles | How much are they? |
| | They're 20 pence each/a packet. |
| | That's 95p altogether. |
| Say what you want | I'd like a packet of crisps. |
| Ask about availability | Have you got any crisps? |
| | Have you got anything to eat? |
| Express hunger | I'm hungry. |
| Express thirst | I'm thirsty. I'd like something to drink. |
| Hurry people | Hurry up! |
| | It's time to go. |

## LESSON 42 What time is it?

| | |
|---|---|
| Ask and tell the time | What time is it? |
| | It's half past five. |
| Ask and talk about schedules | What time does the train leave? |
| | (It leaves) At eight o'clock. |
| Talk about routine | What time is supper? |
| | It's usually at seven. |

## LESSON 43 It's raining.

| | |
|---|---|
| Ask and talk about the weather | What's the weather like? |
| | It's raining. |
| | The sun's shining. |
| | It's very cold. |
| | It's raining. |

## LESSON 44 We have supper at seven.

| | |
|---|---|
| Ask and talk about domestic routine: | |
| times | What time do you get up? |
| | I get up at 7.45. |
| activities | What does she do after breakfast? |
| | She goes riding. |
| meals | What do they have for breakfast? |
| | They have bacon and eggs. |

## LESSON 45 Roundup

## LESSON 46 What's 'goodbye' in Japanese?

| | |
|---|---|
| Ask and talk about words in a foreign language: | What's *goodbye* in Japanese? |
| meaning | It's *sayonara*. |
| | What does *sayonara* mean? |
| | It means *goodbye*. |
| spelling | How do you spell *sayonara*? |
| pronunciation | How do you pronounce *sayonara*? |

## LESSON 47 When's your birthday?

| | |
|---|---|
| Ask and talk about birthdays | When's your birthday? |
| | It's in July. |
| | It's on 4th September. |
| | It's in the summer. |
| Ask and talk about dates | What's the date today? |
| | It's 11th May. |

## LESSON 48 My sister never helps!

| | |
|---|---|
| Ask and talk about jobs in the home | Do you ever make your bed? |
| | Yes, always. |
| Say how often you do things | I never buy comics. |
| Say how often others do things | He always tidies his room. |
| | She sometimes does the washing up. |
| Ask and talk about spending | Do you ever buy sweets? |
| | I sometimes save my pocket money. |

## LESSON 49 Does she like chocolates?

| | |
|---|---|
| Ask and talk about likes and dislikes | Does she like fish? |
| | Yes, she does. |
| | No, she doesn't. |
| | She likes opera but she doesn't like ballet. |
| Ask for and make suggestions | What shall we get her? |
| | Let's get her a plant. |

## LESSON 50 Roundup

Hello. My name's Kate.

And my name's Andy. What's your name?

HIGH TIDE

**1** **Say** hello **and say your name.**

Hello. My name's ....

**2** **Ask your friend's name.**

YOU: What's your name?
FRIEND: My name's ....

**3** **Talk to another friend.**

YOU: Hello. My name's ....
What's your name?
FRIEND: My name's .... Hello.

*Look!*
my name's = my name is
what's = what is

**4** **Listen and repeat.**

0 oh  1 one  2 two  3 three  4 four  5 five
6 six  7 seven  8 eight  9 nine  10 ten

**Rhyme**

Two and four and six and eight.
What's your name? My name is Kate.
One, three, five, seven, nine and ten.
Please, what is your name again?

# Good morning.

**1** **Say** good morning **or** good afternoon **to your teacher.**

Good morning/afternoon, Miss/Mrs/Mr . . . .

**2** **Introduce yourself to a friend.**

YOU:     Hello. I'm . . . .
FRIEND:  I'm . . . . Hello.

**3** **Imagine you are the people in the pictures. Introduce yourself.**

Good morning. My name's Miss Harris. I'm Kate's teacher.

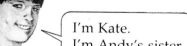

**4** **Copy and complete.**

My name's Kate Morgan.      My . . . . . . . . . Sue.
My brother's name is Andy.   My . . . . . . . . . Miss Harris.

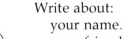

**5** **Write about you.**

Write about:
    your name.
    your friend's name.          your mother's name.
    your teacher's name.         your father's name.

**6** **Say** goodbye **to some friends and to your teacher.**

*Look!*
I'm = I am
my teacher's name = the name of my teacher

(two) 2

# This is my family.

## 🔊 Dialogue

SUE: Hello, Mrs Morgan.
MRS MORGAN: Hello, Sue. How are you?
SUE: I'm OK, thanks.

KATE: Sue, this is my father.
Dad, this is Sue.
She's a friend from school.
SUE: Hello, Mr Morgan.
MR MORGAN: Hello, Sue.

KATE: And this is Andy.
He's my brother. We're twins.
SUE: I know Andy from school. Hello.
ANDY: Hi!

KATE: And this is Lucy.
She's my little sister.
LUCY: I'm a witch! Grr!
KATE: Go away, Lucy.
LUCY: No!
KATE: Yes!

### 1 Greet your friend.

YOU: Hello. How are you?
FRIEND: I'm OK, thanks. How are you?

### 2 🔊 Listen and repeat.

Sue is a friend from school.
She's a friend from school.

Andy is my brother.
He's my brother.

Andy and I are twins.
We're twins.

**4** **Roleplay**

Work in groups. The others in your group are your family. Introduce your family to your teacher.

Mr Green, this is my mother.

**5** **Imagine you are Kate. Write about your family and friends. Start each sentence with** She's**,** He's**, or** We're**.**

1. Lucy          She's ....
2. Andy
3. Andy and I
4. Mr Morgan
5. Mrs Morgan
6. Sue and I

**6** **Introduce two friends to each other.**

YOU:       Anna, this is Robert.
             He's a friend from school.
ANNA:     Hello, Robert.
ROBERT:  Hello, Anna.

**7** **You have a famous friend. Introduce this famous friend to your teacher.**

Miss Harris, this is my friend, Napoleon Bonaparte.

*Look!*
he's = he is
she's = she is
we're = we are

**3** **Talk about each person.**

*1.* She's Kate's mother.

1. *Mrs Morgan*   2. *Mr Morgan*   3. *Andy*

4. *Sue*   5. *John*   6. *Lucy*

# He's called Big Ben.

## 🔊 Dialogue

KATE: This is my cat.

SUE: What's her name?

KATE: Her name's Cleopatra but she's called Cleo.

SUE: Hello, Cleo.

ANDY: And this is our dog. His name's Benjamin but he's called Big Ben.

WOMAN: Sue! Sue! It's tea time.

KATE: Who's that?

SUE: That's my mum. I must go. Goodbye.

KATE: Bye.

**1** Ask and answer about the people and pets below.

YOU: What's his name?

FRIEND: His name's Mr Morgan.

YOU: What's her name?

FRIEND: Her name's Miss Harris.

1. Mr Morgan     4. Mrs Morgan
2. Miss Harris   5. Mr Green
3. Cleopatra     6. Big Ben

1. PRINCE CHARLES
2. KING KONG
3. QUEEN ELIZABETH II
5. TARZAN
4. PRINCESS DIANA
6. STEVIE WONDER

**2** Ask and answer about the people in the pictures.

YOU:   What's his name?
FRIEND:  That's Prince Charles.

**3** Ask about the pictures again.

YOU:   Who's that?
FRIEND:  That's Prince Charles.

**4** Show some photos of your family to your friend.

FRIEND:  Who's that?
YOU:   That's my little sister.
       Her name's Anna.

**5** **Say** goodbye **to a friend.**

YOU:   I must go. Goodbye.
FRIEND:  Bye.

### 📼 Conversation

Complete the conversation with Andy, Kate and Lucy.

ANDY: Hello. I'm Andy. What's your name?
YOU: . . . . . . . . . .
ANDY: This is my twin sister, Kate.
YOU: . . . . . . . . . .
KATE: Hello.
ANDY: And this is my little sister, Lucy.
YOU: . . . . . . . . . .
LUCY: Hello.
ANDY: And this is our dog.
YOU: . . . . . . . . . ?
ANDY: Big Ben. And this is Kate's cat.
YOU: . . . . . . . . . ?
ANDY: Her name's Cleopatra. I must go. Goodbye.
YOU: . . . . . . . . . .

### Read

This is my family: my mother, my father, my brother Andy, my little sister Lucy and me. Andy and I are twins. We have a cat called Cleopatra and a dog called Big Ben.

This is my school. The name of my school is Castle Hill School. My teacher's name is Miss Harris. I have a friend at school. Her name is Sue.

**Complete the sentences.**

Andy is Kate's ... and Lucy is Kate and Andy's .... Big Ben is the ... of the family's ... and Cleopatra is the ... of the family's .... Miss Harris is Kate's ... and Sue is Kate's ....

### Write

Write about your family and school.

## 🖭 Listen

Listen to the people. Who is speaking? Write the
numbers of the pictures in the correct order.

1.

2.

3.
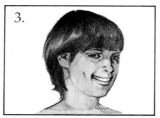

4.

## Quiz

Bring to class some photographs of some famous
people. See if your friends know their names.

---

**Grammar** Lessons 1-5

| *Personal pronouns* | *Possessive adjectives* | *Verb 'to be' Present tense* | |
|---|---|---|---|
| Singular | Singular | Singular | |
| I | my | I'm | = I am |
| you | your | you're | = you are |
| he | his | he's | = he is |
| she | her | she's | = she is |
| it | its | it's | = it is |
| | | | |
| Plural | Plural | Plural | |
| we | our | we're | = we are |
| you | your | you're | = you are |
| they | their | they're | = they are |

| This is | my father.<br>our cat. |
|---|---|

| Who's that? |
|---|

| That's | Cleopatra.<br>my mum. |
|---|---|

| What's | your<br>his<br>her | name? |
|---|---|---|

| My<br>His<br>Her | name's | Kate.<br>Andy.<br>Lucy. |
|---|---|---|

| I<br>We | have a | cat.<br>friend. |
|---|---|---|

| Her name's Cleopatra **but** she's called Cleo. |
|---|

| Andy is Kate's brother **and** Lucy is Kate's sister. |
|---|

| *Definite article 'the'* | *Indefinite article 'a'* | *Genitive apostrophe 's* | *Genitive with 'of'* |
|---|---|---|---|
| **the** name of **the** school | She's **a** friend. | Kate**'s** mother | The name **of** the school |

# How old are you?

## 🎚 Dialogue

LUCY: I want to go on the Flying Octopus!
ANDY: No, Lucy. You're too young!
JOHN: How old are you, Lucy?
ANDY: She's only five.
JOHN: Are you only five, Lucy?
LUCY: No, I'm not. I'm nearly six!
ANDY: Let's go on the Dodgem Cars.
      They're OK. Come on, Lucy.

**1** 🎚 **Listen and repeat.**

11 eleven   12 twelve   13 thirteen
14 fourteen   15 fifteen   16 sixteen
17 seventeen   18 eighteen
19 nineteen   20 twenty

**2** **Ask and answer the questions.**

YOU:    What's 2 + 9 (two and nine)?
FRIEND: 11 (eleven).

1. 2+5    3. 10+3   5. 1+19
2. 6+8    4. 7+12   6. 4+11

**3** **Count like this:**

2,4,6 …
1,3,5 …
20,19,18 …

**7** Say how old the people in the pictures are.

YOU: How old are they?
FRIEND: They're . . . .

1.

2.

Bob (15)
Sarah (10)
Harry (13)

4.

Born 1984

3.

**4** Ask a friend how old he or she is.

YOU: How old are you?
FRIEND: I'm (nearly) . . . ./I'm . . . and a half.

**5** Ask another friend.

YOU: Are you eleven?
FRIEND: Yes, I am./No, I'm not. I'm twelve.

**6** Ask about people in your class.

YOU: How old is . . . ?
FRIEND: He/She's . . . ./I don't know.

**8** Write the ages.

I'm . . . years old.
My brother is . . . .
My sister is . . . .
My best friend is . . . .

# What's your address?

### 📟 Dialogue

SUE: Look at my new address book!
What's your address, Kate?
KATE: It's 65, Cliff Road, Dover.
SUE: And your telephone number?
KATE: It's 38872.
SUE: Say it again slowly.
KATE: Three — double eight — seven — two.
SUE: What's your favourite number?
KATE: Twenty-two. That's the number of our old house.

### 1 📟 Listen and repeat.

| | | | |
|---|---|---|---|
| **20** twenty | **30** thirty | **40** forty | **50** fifty |
| **60** sixty | **70** seventy | **80** eighty | **90** ninety |
| **100** a hundred | **23** twenty-three | **37** thirty-seven | **101** a hundred and one |

### 2 Number buzz

Count round the class. After every four numbers the next person must say *buzz*.

1 2 3 4 BUZZ 6 7 8 9 BUZZ ...

### 3 Work in pairs. Ask and answer the questions.

What's your address?
What's your telephone number?
How old are you?
What's your favourite number?

### 4 Copy and complete.

My name is . . . .
I am . . . years old.
My address is . . . .
My telephone number is . . . .
My favourite number is . . . .

### 5 Write about Sue and John.

Her name is Sue Wilson. She is . . . .

Name: Sue Wilson
Age: 12
Address: 41, Stratton Street, Dover
Telephone: Dover 50987

Name: John Dawson
Age: 12
Address: 32, Castle Street, Dover
Telephone: Dover 66221

### 6 Look it up!

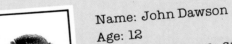

| | |
|---|---|
| Green S, 17 Blenheim Road, Dover | Dover 17902 |
| Green S, 92 Albert Park Road, Dover | Dover 36149 |
| Green S, 12 Queens Road, Dover | Dover 42691 |
| Harris A W, 323 Manor Road, Dover | Dover 62271 |
| Harris B, 12 Brook Road, Dover | Dover 57418 |
| Harris B, 58 Chesterfield Drive, Dover | Dover 82790 |

Miss Harris's address is 12, Brook Road, Dover.
What's her telephone number?
Mr Green's telephone number is Dover 36149.
What's his address?

# What's this?

## 🔲 Dialogue

ANDY:  Go away, Lucy.

LUCY:  What's this?
ANDY:  What?
LUCY:  This. Is it a ruler?
ANDY:  No, it isn't. It's a calculator.

LUCY:  What's that?
ANDY:  It's a cassette recorder. Now go away.

**1**  **Ask and answer about the pictures below.**

YOU:  What's picture 1?
FRIEND:  It's a ruler.

1. ruler
2. pencil
3. comic
4. pen
5. notebook
6. desk
7. stool
8. calculator
9. rubber
10. computer

**2**  **Look again at the pictures in exercise 1. Ask and answer the questions.**

*Picture 1*
YOU:  What's this? Is it a ruler?
FRIEND:  Yes, it is.

*Picture 2*
YOU:  What's this? Is it a pen?
FRIEND:  No, it isn't. It's a pencil.

1. a ruler?
2. a pen?
3. a comic?
4. a pencil?
5. a notebook?
6. a table?
7. a chair?
8. a computer?
9. a rubber?
10. a computer?

*Look!*

What's **this**?

What's **that**?

# It's an African elephant.

1. BALD EAGLE (NORTH AMERICA)

2. SHEEP DOG (ENGLAND)

3. PANDA (CHINA)

4. LION (AFRICA)

5. ELEPHANT (AFRICA)

6. TIGER (INDIA)

## 📼 Dialogue

MR GREEN: Look at the picture on page thirty-five. Andy, what's this animal?
ANDY: It's an elephant.
MR GREEN: I know it's an elephant! But where is it from?
ANDY: India.
MR GREEN: No, you're wrong. It's from Africa. It's an African elephant. Look at its big ears. Now look at the next picture. What's this animal?
ANDY: I know. It's an Indian tiger.
MR GREEN: Good! Thank you, Andy.

### Countries and nationalities

| | |
|---|---|
| Africa | African |
| America | American |
| China | Chinese |
| England | English |
| India | Indian |

**1** Ask and say what the animals are.

YOU: What's this animal?
FRIEND: It's a bald eagle.

**2** Ask and say what country the animals are from.

YOU: Where is it from?
FRIEND: It's from North America.
It's an American bald eagle.

**3** Draw or trace each animal and write about it.

This eagle is from North America.

> **Look!**
>
> **a** sheep dog **an** elephant
> **an** English sheep dog **an** African elephant

### Did you know?

The elephant is the only animal with four knees.

(fourteen) 14

## 📼 Conversation

Complete the conversation with Kate.

KATE: Hello. How are you?

YOU: ......... ?

KATE: I'm fine thanks. Look at this. It's my new address book. What's your name?

YOU: .........

KATE: And your address?

YOU: .........

KATE: How old are you?

YOU: .........

KATE: I'm eleven. My brother Andy's eleven too. We're twins. Are you a twin?

YOU: .........

KATE: What's your favourite number?

YOU: .........

KATE: My favourite number is twenty-two. The number of our old house was twenty-two. I must go now. Bye!

YOU: .........

## Read

This is Mr Green's class. Andy is one of Mr Green's students. Mr Green is a very good teacher. Andy has a pencil, a rubber and a book on his desk. Today the lesson is about wild animals. The picture of the African elephant is on page thirty-five of Andy's book. The elephant is nearly twelve years old.

## Correct these statements.

1. Andy is a teacher in Mr Green's class.
2. He has a pen, a pencil and a book on his desk.
3. The lesson is about pets.
4. The animals are on page thirty-six of Andy's book.
5. The elephant is from India.
6. The elephant is twelve years old.

## Write

Write about your school. Copy and complete the sentences.

The name of my school is ....
My class is called Class ....
The name of my English teacher is ....
... is a ... good teacher.

## 📻 Listen

Listen and write the names of the animals in the order in which you hear them.

## Project

Find out the names of:
- a big city in India.
- a wild animal from India.
- a country in Africa.
- a wild animal from Africa.
- a big city in China.
- a wild animal from China.

### Grammar Lessons 6-10

| How old | are | you? they? | I'm They're He's She's | twelve (years old). |
|---|---|---|---|---|
|  | is | he? she? |  |  |

| Are you eleven? | Yes, I am. |
|---|---|
|  | No, I'm not. |

| What's this/that? | It's | a ruler. an elephant. an Indian tiger. |
|---|---|---|

| Is it a ruler? | Yes, it is. |
|---|---|
|  | No, it isn't. |

| Where is it from? | It's from | Africa. India. England. | He She | has a book on | his her | desk. |
|---|---|---|---|---|---|---|

*Demonstrative pronoun*
What's **this/that**?

*Demonstrative adjective*
What's **this/that** animal?

# He's American.

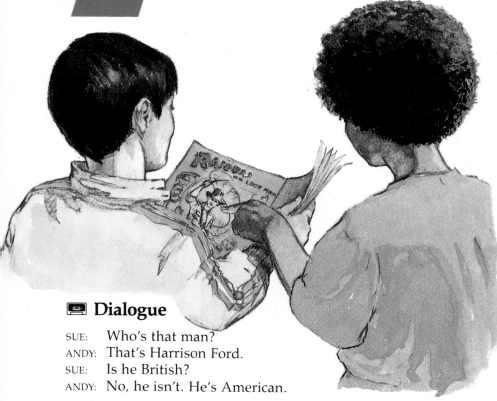

**Countries and nationalities**

| Britain | British |
|---|---|
| France | French |
| Italy | Italian |
| Spain | Spanish |
| The United States of America (USA) | American |

**1** Ask and answer about the people in the pictures below.

YOU: Who's that woman?
FRIEND: That's Isabelle Huppert.
YOU: Where's she from?
FRIEND: She's from France.
YOU: Who's that man?
FRIEND: That's Severiano Ballesteros.
YOU: Where's he from?
FRIEND: He's from Spain.

🔊 **Dialogue**

SUE: Who's that man?
ANDY: That's Harrison Ford.
SUE: Is he British?
ANDY: No, he isn't. He's American.

2. SEVERIANO BALLESTEROS (SPAIN)

3. EDDIE MURPHY (USA)

1. ISABELLE HUPPERT (FRANCE)

**2** Ask and answer about nationality.

YOU: Is he British?
FRIEND: No, he isn't.
He's American.

YOU: Is she Italian?
FRIEND: Yes, she is.

Now ask about the people below:

1. French?   3. American?   5. Spanish?
2. Italian?   4. French?   6. British?

**3** Ask and say what nationality you are.

YOU: What nationality are you?
FRIEND: I'm . . . .

**4** Write about the men and women in the pictures.

1. The woman in picture one is Isabelle Huppert. She's French.
2. The man in picture two is . . . .

**5** What is hello **and** thank you **in**:

French?
Spanish?
Chinese?

**4. SOPHIA LOREN (ITALY)**

**5. HARRISON FORD (USA)**

**6. DALEY THOMPSON (BRITAIN)**

# We're from Penzance.

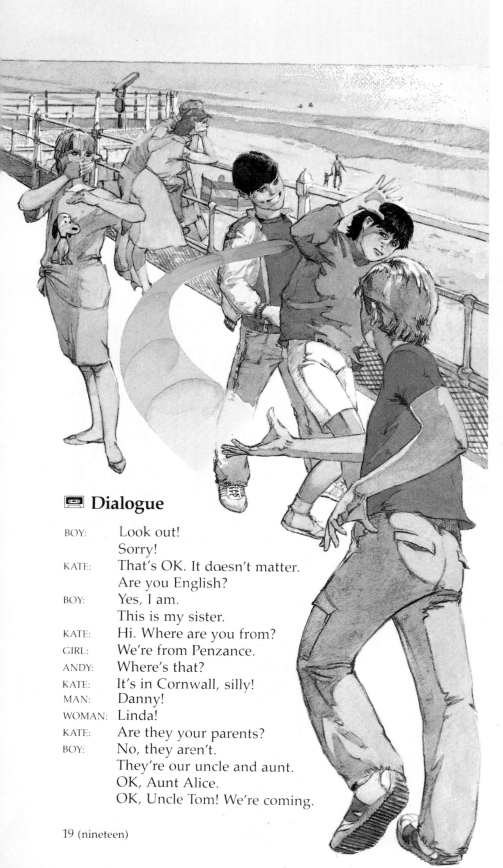

**1. BUENOS AIRES (ARGENTINA)**

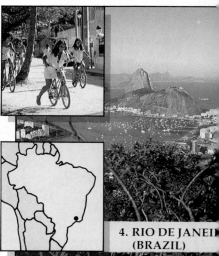

**4. RIO DE JANEI (BRAZIL)**

## 🖭 Dialogue

| | |
|---|---|
| BOY: | Look out! |
| | Sorry! |
| KATE: | That's OK. It doesn't matter. |
| | Are you English? |
| BOY: | Yes, I am. |
| | This is my sister. |
| KATE: | Hi. Where are you from? |
| GIRL: | We're from Penzance. |
| ANDY: | Where's that? |
| KATE: | It's in Cornwall, silly! |
| MAN: | Danny! |
| WOMAN: | Linda! |
| KATE: | Are they your parents? |
| BOY: | No, they aren't. |
| | They're our uncle and aunt. |
| | OK, Aunt Alice. |
| | OK, Uncle Tom! We're coming. |

**Countries and nationalities**

| | |
|---|---|
| Argentina | Argentinian |
| Brazil | Brazilian |
| Germany | German |
| Greece | Greek |
| Japan | Japanese |
| Turkey | Turkish |

**1** **Talk to the people in the pictures.**

| | |
|---|---|
| YOU: | Where are you from? |
| FRIEND: | We're from Buenos Aires. |
| YOU: | Where's that? |
| FRIEND: | It's in Argentina. |

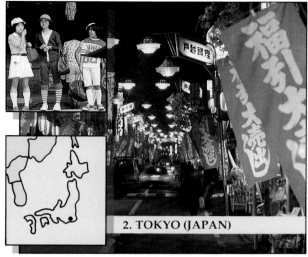

2. TOKYO (JAPAN)

3. ISTANBUL (TURKEY)

5. ATHENS (GREECE)

6. MUNICH (GERMANY)

**2** **Talk to the people again.**

1. YOU:    Are you Argentinian?
   FRIEND:  Yes, we are.

2. YOU:    Are you Chinese?
   FRIEND:  No, we aren't. We're
           Japanese.

3. Turkish?  5. Greek?
4. French?   6. Spanish?

**3** **Write about the people.**

The girls in picture one are from Buenos Aires
in Argentina.
The boys . . . .
The children . . . .

**4** **Say what nationality you and your friends
are, which town you are from and which
country.**

We're . . . .
We're from . . . , in . . . .

```
Look!

1 boy — 2 boys
1 girl — 2 girls
1 child — 2 children
1 man — 2 men
1 woman — 2 women
```

(twenty) 20

# Do you want a sweet?

### 🔲 Dialogue

KATE: Do you want a sweet?
GIRL: Yes, please.
KATE: Here you are.
GIRL: Thanks very much.
KATE: Do you want one?
BOY: What is it?
KATE: It's liquorice.
BOY: No, thanks. I hate liquorice.
GIRL: We must go now.
Thanks for the sweet.
KATE: That's OK. Bye.

**1** **Offer and accept.**

YOU: Do you want a.../some ...?
FRIEND: Yes, please.
YOU: Here you are.
FRIEND: Thank you./Thanks.

*a sweet*     *some sweets*

*a crisp*     *some crisps*

*a chocolate*     *some chocolates*

*an icecream*     *some chewing gum*

**2** **Offer and refuse.**

YOU: Do you want a .../some ...?
FRIEND: No, thanks.

**3** **Offer and accept or refuse.**

YOU: Do you want some liquorice?
FRIEND: Yes, please. I love liquorice./
No, thanks. I hate liquorice.

**4** **Thank your friend for the icecream,
the crisps and the chewing gum.**

YOU: Thanks for the ....
FRIEND: That's OK.

**5** **Write and thank a friend for the following:**

Thank you very much for the ....

# What colour are your eyes?

What colour is your hair? What colour are your eyes?
What are your favourite colours?

| Name: | Kate | Lucy | Andy | John | Cleopatra |
|---|---|---|---|---|---|
| Hair: | black | blonde | black | dark brown | Its fur is black and white |
| Eyes: | brown | blue | brown | grey | light green |
| Favourite colours: | blue and bright pink | red and bright yellow | green and orange | blue and purple | |

**1** **Ask and answer about the people.**

YOU:     What colour is Kate's hair?
FRIEND: It's black.
YOU:     What colour are Kate's eyes?
FRIEND: They're brown.
YOU:     What are her favourite colours?
FRIEND: They're blue and bright pink.

**2** **Write about each person.**

Kate:
Her hair is black, her eyes are brown and her favourite colours are blue and bright pink.

**3** **Write about yourself.**

My hair is ....

**4** **Think of someone in the class. Answer your partner's questions.**

FRIEND: Is it a he or a she?/Is it a boy or a girl?
YOU:     It's a he./It's a boy.
FRIEND: Is his hair black?
YOU:     Yes, it is.
FRIEND: Are his eyes blue?
YOU:     No, they aren't. They're brown.

**5** **Quiz**

Write down the answers. You have one minute!
What colour is ... ?

*a panda*

*an apple*

*a cloud*

*a tomato*

*the sea*

*grass*

*an elephant*

*an orange*

*the sun*

*a banana*

*the sky*

*a tree*

**Remember! Some can be more than one colour.**

# Roundup

## 🔊 Conversation

Look at the information about Linda, then complete the conversation with her. Ask her questions.

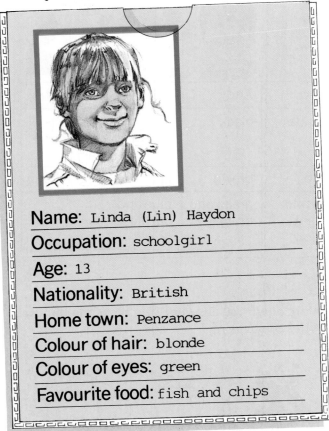

**Name:** Linda (Lin) Haydon

**Occupation:** schoolgirl

**Age:** 13

**Nationality:** British

**Home town:** Penzance

**Colour of hair:** blonde

**Colour of eyes:** green

**Favourite food:** fish and chips

LINDA: Hello.
YOU: Hello. ...?
LINDA: Linda Haydon.
YOU: OK, Linda ...?
LINDA: I'm thirteen.
YOU: .........?
LINDA: Yes, I am.
YOU: .........?
LINDA: From Penzance, in Cornwall.
YOU: .........?
LINDA: Fish and chips.

**Talk to your partner in the same way and make a chart.**

## Read

### New singer for Menudo

Robert is a new member of the band Menudo. He is called 'Bobby' by his friends. He is American. He was born in the USA but his family are from Puerto Rico. He is nearly 15 years old. He is good-looking. His hair is brown and his eyes are blue. His favourite food is icecream, chocolates and crisps.

**Answer the questions.**

1. What is the boy called by his friends?
   a) Bob  b) Robby  c) Bobby

2. What nationality is he?
   a) British  b) American  c) Puerto Rican

3. Where are his family from?
   a) Puerto Rico  b) The USA  c) Britain

4. How old is he?
   a) fifteen  b) sixteen  c) fourteen

5. What colour are his hair and eyes?
   a) His hair is brown and his eyes are blue.
   b) They're brown.
   c) His hair is black and his eyes are blue.

6. What is his favourite food?
   a) chocolate crisps
   b) chocolate icecream and crisps
   c) chocolates, icecream and crisps

## Write

Look at the information about Linda and the reading text about Robert. Write a paragraph about Linda.

**Begin like this:** Linda is a schoolgirl. She is called ....

## 🔊 Listen

Listen to the results of the British Grand Prix on the radio. Copy the chart on the right and complete it with the colour of the cars and the nationality of the drivers.

## Project

Find out the countries where these cars come from:

| Citroen | Volkswagen | Jaguar | Buick |
|---------|-----------|--------|-------|
| Seat | Alfa Romeo | Toyota | Volvo |

| NAME | NATIONALITY | MODEL | COLOUR |
|------|-------------|-------|--------|
| Moreno | | McLaren | |
| Gabon | | Ferrari | |
| Scott | | Renault | |
| Marshall | | Alfa Romeo | |

## Grammar Lessons 11-15

*Verb 'to be'*
Singular

| Am I | | American? |
|------|--|-----------|
| Are you | | |
| Is he/she | | |

| Yes, | I am. |
|------|-------|
| | you are. |
| | he/she is. |

| No, | I'm not. |
|-----|----------|
| | you aren't. |
| | he/she isn't. |

Plural

| Are | we you they | English? |
|-----|-------------|----------|

| Yes, | we you they | are. |
|------|-------------|------|

| No, | we you they | aren't. |
|-----|-------------|---------|

| What colour | is | his | hair? |
|-------------|-----|-----|-------|
| | are | her | eyes? |

| It's black. |
|-------------|
| They're blue. |

| I | love hate | sweets. chewing gum. |
|---|-----------|----------------------|

| Do you want | | an orange? |
|-------------|--|------------|
| | some | chewing gum? crisps? |

| *Singular* | *Plural* | *Singular* | *Plural* |
|-----------|----------|-----------|----------|
| a boy | some boys | a sweet | some sweets |
| a girl | some girls | a chocolate | some chocolates |
| a child | some children | a crisp | some crisps |
| a man | some men | | |
| a woman | some women | | |

# Whose sweater is this?

jeans

sweater

KATE'S CLOTHES

boots

T-shirt

anorak

trousers

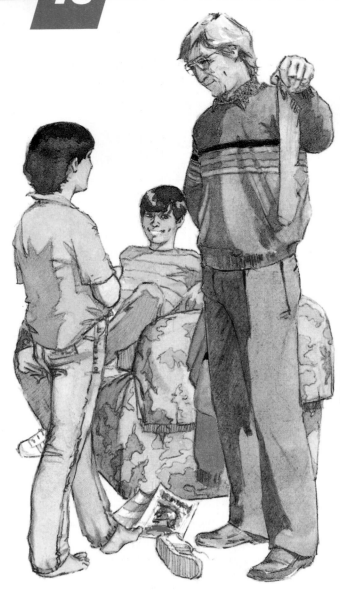

### 📼 Dialogue

MR MORGAN: Kate, whose sweater is this?
Is it yours or Andy's?
KATE: It's Sue's.
MR MORGAN: Well, why is it here?
KATE: I don't know.
MR MORGAN: And whose socks are these?
Are these yours, Andy?
ANDY: Mine? Pink socks?
KATE: Well, they aren't mine.
ANDY: Perhaps they're yours, Dad.
MR MORGAN: Don't be cheeky!

MRS MORGAN'S CLOTHES

blouse

shoes

ANDY'S CLOTHES

*trainers*

*socks*

*jacket*

*skirt*

MR MORGAN'S CLOTHES

*shirt*

*dress*

*coat*

**1** **Look at the pictures. Ask and answer. Choose different clothes each time.**

YOU:     Whose sweater is this?
FRIEND:  It's Andy's.
YOU:     Whose boots are these?
FRIEND:  They're Kate's.

*Look!*

| It's | my<br>your<br>his<br>her | sweater. | It's | mine.<br>yours.<br>his.<br>hers. |

**2** **Use the groups of clothes to complete the conversation.**

MRS MORGAN:  Is this Andy's T-shirt?
KATE:           No, it isn't his. It's mine.
MRS MORGAN:  Are these Kate's trainers?
ANDY:          No, they aren't hers. They're mine.
MRS MORGAN:  Are these Kate's jeans?
ANDY:          ..........
MRS MORGAN:  Is this Andy's jacket?
KATE:           ..........
MRS MORGAN:  Are these Andy's boots?
KATE:           ..........
MRS MORGAN:  Is this Kate's sweater?
ANDY:          ..........
MRS MORGAN:  Is this your dress, Kate?
KATE:           ..........
MRS MORGAN:  Is this your blouse, Kate?
KATE:           ..........

**3** **Collect a few clothes and school things like pens and pencils. Hold up something and ask whose it is.**

YOU:     Whose jacket is this?
FRIEND:  It's mine.

# Who's your favourite star?

## 🔊 Dialogue

JOHN: Who's that?
SUE: That's Robert Power.
I think he's great.
Who's your favourite pop star?
JOHN: I don't know. I don't like
pop music much.
SUE: You are funny!
KATE: I like Bob Marley.
SUE: Yes, I like him too. And I also like
Tracey Ullman.
KATE: Oh, I don't like her. I think
she's horrible. Hey, is that a picture of
Wham!?
SUE: Yes, it is.
KATE: I like their new record.
SUE: I don't like it. I think it's boring.
JOHN: You're boring, you two. I'm going home.
See you!

> *Look!*
>
> I like Simon Le Bon. = I like **him**.
> I don't like Tracey Ullman. = I don't like **her**.
> I like Duran Duran. = I like **them**.
> I don't like their record. = I don't like **it**.

### 1 Ask and answer.

YOU: Who's your favourite pop star or band?
FRIEND: I like ....
YOU: Yes, I like him/her/them too./
I don't like him/her/them.

### 2 Ask and answer.

FRIEND: What's your favourite record?
YOU: I like the new record by ....
FRIEND: Yes, I like it too./I don't like it.

### 3 Say what you think about famous people.

| fantastic | horrible |
|-----------|----------|
| great | boring |
| good | bad |

I think David Bowie is fantastic.
I think their new record is bad.
I think they're great.

### 4 Copy and complete.

| Favourite male pop star | |
|---|---|
| Favourite female pop star | |
| Favourite band | |
| Favourite record in the Top Ten | |

**Look at your friend's notes and compare them with yours.**

### 5 Write about your favourites.

I like .... I think he/she's ....
I also like .... I think they're ....
My favourite record is ....

### 🔲 Dialogue

ANDY: Have you got a bike?
JOHN: Yes, I have. Have you?
ANDY: Yes, I've got a BMX.
JOHN: I've got one, too. What colour's yours?
ANDY: Mine's gold with black wheels.
It's over there.
JOHN: Great! Let's see it.

**1** **Look at the pictures. Ask and answer about your possessions.**

YOU:  Have you got a bike?
FRIEND: Yes, I have. Have you?
YOU:  No, I haven't./Yes, I have.

*a bike*
*a camera*
*a watch*
*a tennis racket*
*a football*
*a stamp album*
*a radio*
*a tent*
*a pet*
*a sleeping bag*

**2** **Talk about your possessions with a friend.**

YOU:  I've got a camera.
FRIEND: Yes, I've got one too./I haven't got one.

**3** **Write one sentence about some things you've got and one sentence about some things you haven't got.**

I've got a watch, an old bike and a radio.
I haven't got a football or a tent.

**4** **Wordsearch**

| A | C | E | F | S | H | J | L |
|---|---|---|---|---|---|---|---|
| R | P | W | A | T | C | H | N |
| T | X | V | Z | A | B | D | F |
| E | A | R | E | M | A | C | I |
| K | K | M | O | P | Q | S | T |
| I | A | D | R | A | D | I | O |
| B | N | K | H | L | Z | Y | U |
| F | O | O | T | B | A | L | L |
| Q | T | U | E | U | W | Y | R |
| C | D | S | P | M | Z | O | M |

Look at the word puzzle above and find the names of six other things from the pictures on the left. The words can go forwards (→) backwards (←) up (↑) or down (↓). You can use letters more than once.

> **Look!**
> I've = I have
> I haven't = I have not

# How many have you got?

| | KATE | JOHN | YOU |
|---|---|---|---|
| FOREIGN STAMPS | ✓ (nearly 200) | ✗ | |
| FOREIGN COINS | ✗ | ✗ | |
| BADGES | ✓ (8) | ✓ (12) | |
| POSTCARDS | ✓ (57) | ✗ | |
| STICKERS | ✗ | ✓ (30) | |
| POP STAR PHOTOS | ✓ (11) | ✗ | |
| POSTERS | ✓ (5) | ✓ (6) | |
| MODEL TRAINS | ✗ | ✓ | |
| ANY OTHER COLLECTIONS | ✓ (shells) | ✗ | |

### 🔊 Dialogue

SUE: How many postcards have you got?
KATE: About fifty.
SUE: My cousin's got nearly a hundred.
KATE: Has she got any 3D postcards?
SUE: Yes, she has. They're terrific.

**1** Look at the chart of people's collections, put a tick (✔) for yes and the number of things in your collection, or put a cross (✘) for no.

| Look! | | | |
|---|---|---|---|
| hasn't = has not | | | |
| I've | got | | some postcards. |
| I haven't | | any | postcards. |
| Have you | | | postcards? |

**2** Ask and answer about your collections.

YOU: Have you got any foreign stamps?
FRIEND: Yes, I have.
YOU: How many have you got?
FRIEND: Nearly three hundred.
YOU: Have you got any foreign coins?
FRIEND: No, I haven't.

**3** Ask and answer about Kate and John.

YOU: Has Kate got any foreign stamps?
FRIEND: Yes, she has. She's got nearly two hundred.
YOU: Has she got any foreign coins?
FRIEND: No, she hasn't.

**4** Write about collections.

Kate's got some stamps, some badges, some postcards, some photos of pop stars, some posters and some shells. She hasn't got any foreign coins, stickers or model trains.

John's got …
My friend's got …
I've got …

**5** Picture puzzle

Take the first letter of each of the following and see what Andy collects.

1.    2.    3.    4.

5.    6.

## 📼 Conversation

Complete the conversation with Andy.

ANDY: Hello.
YOU: ..........
ANDY: How are you?
YOU: ..........
ANDY: Do you know, I've got three uncles, two aunts and ten cousins. What about you?
YOU: ..........
ANDY: Who's your favourite pop band?
YOU: ..........
ANDY: Yes, I like them too. I think they're great. And I like Michael Jackson.
YOU: ..........
ANDY: Have you got any collections?
YOU: ..........
ANDY: I've got six wild life posters. Well, I'm going home now. Bye!
YOU: ..........

## 📼 Listen

Listen to Jessica. Write the numbers of the topics below in the order in which she talks about them.

1. Her pets
2. Her family
3. Her collections
4. Her favourite clothes
5. Her opinion of Michael Jackson

## Read

**H**is name is Michael Jackson — super- super- super-star! Have you got any Michael Jackson songs? Perhaps you've got one of his hit albums or videos. Millions of people all over the world like Michael Jackson.

Michael has got three sisters and five brothers. The boys are all in the band called The Jackson Five, but Michael is the international superstar. Why do people like him? They like his music, they like his songs and they like his dancing. They even like his clothes: his boots covered with sequins, the silver glove on his left hand, and his blue and gold sequinned jacket and black trousers.

On stage Michael is a star but at home he is quiet and shy. He lives in a very big house in Encino, California with his mother, Katherine, and two of his sisters, Janet and La Toya. He loves animals. He's got lots of animals in his private zoo, including an eight-foot long boa constrictor snake called Muscles and a sheep called Mr Tibbs.

### Michael Jackson quiz

1. Who are The Jackson Five?
2. How many sisters has Michael Jackson got?
3. Who is Katharine?
4. Who are Janet and La Toya?
5. Where are Michael Jackson's animals?
6. What is Muscles?
7. What is Mr Tibbs?

## Write

Write sentences about your family. Say how many brothers and sisters you've got and what their names are.

Write about your collections or pets. Say what they are.

Write about your favourite clothes and what colour they are.

Write about your favourite pop stars and music.

## Swap Shop

Make a list of things you have got but you don't want. Then make another list of things you want but you haven't got. With your friends, see how many things you can swap, like this:

'Who wants to swap ... for ... ?'

---

### Grammar Lessons 16-20

| Possessive pronouns | Object pronouns |
|---|---|
| mine | me |
| yours | you |
| his | him |
| hers | her |
| its | it |
| ours | us |
| theirs | them |

| Whose | sweater is this? |
|---|---|
| | socks are these? |

| It's mine. |
|---|
| They're his. |

| Yes, | I | have. |
|---|---|---|
| No, | | haven't. |

| Have you | got | a camera? |
|---|---|---|
| Has he/she | | any stamps? |

| Yes, | he/she | has. |
|---|---|---|
| No, | | hasn't. |

| I've | got | a camera. |
|---|---|---|
| I haven't | | one. |

| I've got some | stamps. |
|---|---|
| I haven't got any | |

| I | like | Tracey Ullman. |
|---|---|---|
| | don't like | Simon Le Bon. |
| | | Duran Duran. |
| | | their new record. |

| I think | she's | great. |
|---|---|---|
| | he's | boring. |
| | they're | good. |
| | it's | bad. |

# How many are there?

**Dialogue**

KATE: Guess what!
ANDY: What?
KATE: There are twenty-two people with brown hair in my class.
ANDY: That's a lot. How many are there in your class altogether?
KATE: Only thirty!

CASTLE HILL SCHOOL

Class: 1A
Total number of students: 30
Number of girls: 17
Number of boys: 13

**1** **Look at the class record book. Ask and answer about Kate's class.**

How many students are there in Kate's class altogether?
There are ... students.
        ... girls.
        ... boys.

**2** **Ask and answer about your class.**

**CLASS 1A**

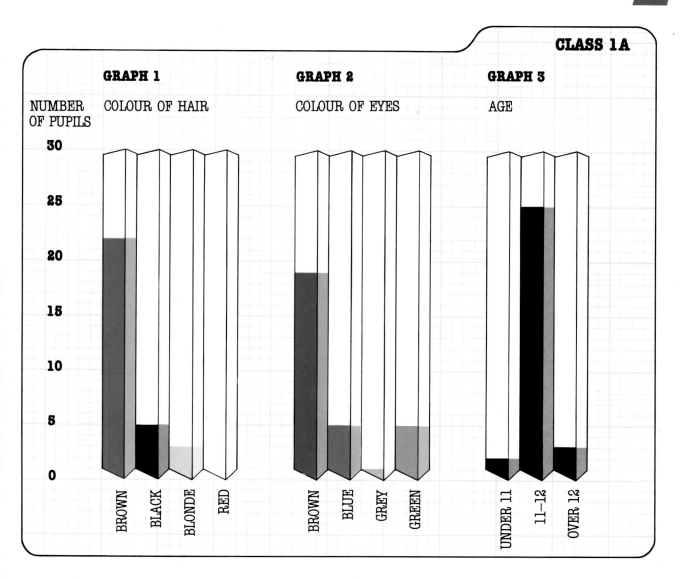

**GRAPH 1**

NUMBER OF PUPILS    COLOUR OF HAIR

BROWN  BLACK  BLONDE  RED

**GRAPH 2**

COLOUR OF EYES

BROWN  BLUE  GREY  GREEN

**GRAPH 3**

AGE

UNDER 11  11–12  OVER 12

**3** **Ask and answer questions from the graphs.**

*Graph 1*
YOU:     How many students are there with brown hair?
FRIEND:  There are twenty-two.

*Graph 2*
YOU:     How many students are there with brown eyes?
FRIEND:  There are nineteen.

*Graph 3*
YOU:     How many students are there under eleven years old?
FRIEND:  There are ....

**4** **Ask and answer more questions.**

*Graph 1*
YOU:     Are there any students with brown hair?
FRIEND:  Yes, there are.
YOU:     Are there any students with red hair?
FRIEND:  No, there aren't.

**5** **Make your own class graphs and write about them.**

Hair: In my class there are ... students with ... hair, ... with ... hair and ....

Eyes: There are ....

Age: There are ....

# There's an attic.

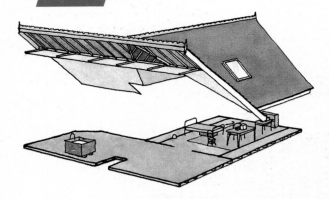

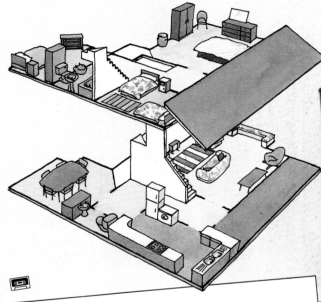

**Our house**

Our house is quite big. There are two floors and an attic. Downstairs on the ground floor there is a sitting room, a dining room, a kitchen and a toilet. Up-stairs on the next floor there is a bath-room and three bedrooms. The big bedroom is my parents' room. Kate and Lucy's room is opposite theirs. My bedroom is the small one. Our play room is in the attic in the roof. That's the best room in the house.

### 1 Read and answer.

1. How many rooms are there downstairs?
2. How many bedrooms are there upstairs?
3. Whose is the big bedroom?
4. Where is Kate and Lucy's bedroom?
5. Whose is the small bedroom?
6. Where is the play room?

### 2 Ask and answer about the rooms.

YOU:      Is there a kitchen on the ground floor?
FRIEND:  Yes, there is.

YOU:      Is there a kitchen on the next floor?
FRIEND:  No, there isn't

| | | |
|---|---|---|
| 1. kitchen | 4. bedroom | 6. toilet |
| 2. play room | 5. dining room | 7. bathroom |
| 3. sitting room | | |

### 3 In pairs, ask each other about rooms in your homes.

### 4 Where am I?

You are in one of the rooms of the house. Write down the name of the room and give it to your teacher. Your friends must guess where you are.

FRIEND 1:  Are you in the bathroom?
YOU:        No, I'm not.
FRIEND 2:  Are you in the big bedroom?

*Look!*

my parents' room = the room of my parents.

# Spiders in the chimney.

The attic is our favourite room. It's at the top of the house. There are some stairs up to it and a very small door. There's a notice on the door saying 'PRIVATE'.

The attic is dark and a bit spooky. Lucy's afraid of it but I'm not. I like it because it's ~~ourts~~ ours.

There are lots of things in it. There's an old bed next to the wall. There's a desk, a big table and some chairs next to the window. There are some spiders and a bird's nest in the chimney.

In the corner there's an enormous cupboard. It's full of games, old toys, dolls and clothes.

On the walls there are lots of flags, and posters, and some photos of pop stars and my favourite football team. There's also a picture of Big Ben by Lucy. (It's ~~horible~~ horrible.)

There aren't any curtains but there's an old red carpet on the floor. Under the bed there's a big black box with a lock for my models and badges.

I like the attic best when I'm alone in it.

\* \* \* \* \* \* \* \* \* \* \*

**2** Answer these questions about the attic. Use:

| | |
|---|---|
| Yes, there is. | No, there isn't. |
| Yes, there are. | No, there aren't. |

Is there a bed in the room?
    a typewriter on the bed?
    a carpet on the floor?
    a box under the table?
    a bird's nest in the chimney?

Are there any curtains?
    any chairs?
    any models on the table?
    any spiders on the bed?
    any posters on the walls?

**3** Say where everything is. Answer these questions. Use:

in          next to

on          under

Where is the bed?
    the bird's nest?
    the cupboard?
    the typewriter?
    the carpet?
    the box?
    the notice saying 'PRIVATE'?

Where are the table and chairs?
    the posters?
    Andy's models?

**Rhyme**

I know a house
It's a nice old house.
It's a nice old house
In a square.
And in that house
There's a funny old ghost
And he's just behind
Your chair.
Aaagh!

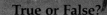

**1** True or False?

1. The attic has got a very big door.
2. Lucy likes the attic.
3. There are lots of things in the attic.
4. There is a bed next to the window.
5. There are some chairs in the room.
6. There aren't any posters on the wall.
7. There is a picture of Cleopatra.
8. There aren't any curtains.
9. There is a big black box in the cupboard.

# I live in Dover.

Kate is writing a letter to her new penfriend. Her name is Rachel Jones and she lives in Australia.

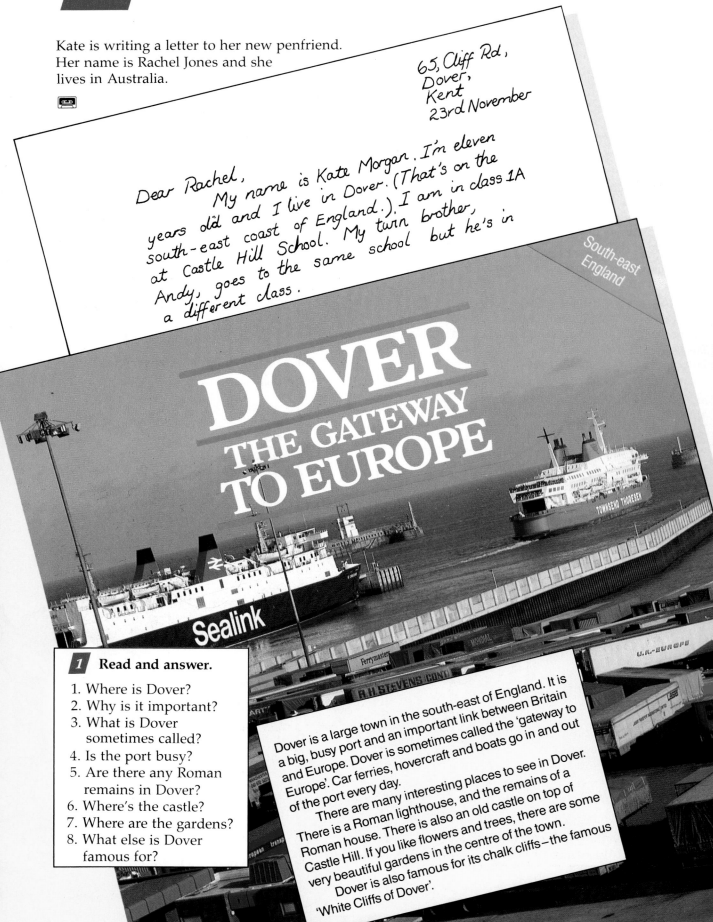

> 65, Cliff Rd,
> Dover,
> Kent
> 23rd November
>
> Dear Rachel,
>     My name is Kate Morgan. I'm eleven years old and I live in Dover. (That's on the south-east coast of England.) I am in class 1A at Castle Hill School. My twin brother, Andy, goes to the same school but he's in a different class.

South-east England

## DOVER THE GATEWAY TO EUROPE

Sealink

### 1 Read and answer.

1. Where is Dover?
2. Why is it important?
3. What is Dover sometimes called?
4. Is the port busy?
5. Are there any Roman remains in Dover?
6. Where's the castle?
7. Where are the gardens?
8. What else is Dover famous for?

Dover is a large town in the south-east of England. It is a big, busy port and an important link between Britain and Europe. Dover is sometimes called the 'gateway to Europe'. Car ferries, hovercraft and boats go in and out of the port every day.

There are many interesting places to see in Dover. There is a Roman lighthouse, and the remains of a Roman house. There is also an old castle on top of Castle Hill. If you like flowers and trees, there are some very beautiful gardens in the centre of the town. Dover is also famous for its chalk cliffs – the famous 'White Cliffs of Dover'.

**2** Look at this map of Britain. Say where the towns are.

Southampton is in the south/on the south coast of England.

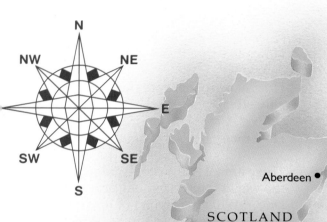

**3** Look at the notes about Dover and write similar information about two large towns in your country.

| NAME OF TOWN | Dover |
|---|---|
| SITUATION | south-east of England |
| PLACES TO SEE | the 'White Cliffs of Dover' a castle some gardens |
| HISTORICAL REMAINS | a Roman lighthouse the remains of a Roman house |

**4** Write a few sentences about the two towns.

… is a large town in …. There are many interesting places to …. There is …. There are also some/many ….

**5** Ask and answer.

YOU: Where do you live?
FRIEND: I live in the centre of ….. That's in the north of …. I live near ….

**6** Write about your friend.

My friend lives in ….

*Look!*

in the north of England
on the south coast of Britain
in the centre of London

**▭ Rhyme**

In the north, in the south, in the east,
  in the west,
Wherever you live, your home is the best.

## Read

Read the description of the house, trace the diagram and then complete it.

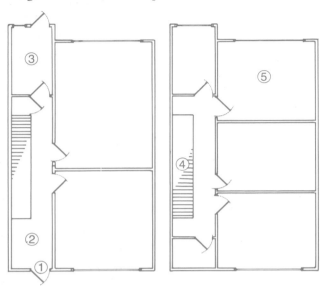

**Ground floor**
① Front door
② Hall
③ Kitchen

**First floor**
④ Stairs
⑤ Play room

This house is quite big. There are two floors. Downstairs there's a sitting-room on the right, and next to the sitting-room is a dining room. There's a kitchen opposite the front door, next to the dining room. There's a small toilet under the stairs. Upstairs there are three bedrooms, a play room and a bathroom. Two of the bedrooms are quite big. The small bedroom is over the kitchen and the bathroom is at the top of the stairs, over the hall.

## 🔊 Listen

Listen to this radio advertisement
Write down the rooms the person describes.

## Write

Write a few sentences describing:

1. Your house/flat and your bedroom.
2. Your school and your classroom.

**Begin like this:**
Our flat is quite small. There are . . . .

## 🔊 Conversation

Complete the conversation with Kate.

KATE: Hello. How are you?
YOU: . . . . . . . . .
KATE: Guess what! There are only four people with blonde hair in my class.
How many are there in your class?
YOU: . . . . . . . . .
KATE: How many people are there in your class altogether?
YOU: . . . . . . . . .
KATE: How many boys and how many girls?
YOU: . . . . . . . . .
KATE: There are lots of posters and pictures on the wall in our classroom, and a map of Dover. What have you got on your classroom walls?
YOU: . . . . . . . . .
KATE: I know a joke about spiders. What's black, hairy and horrible, with eight legs, and says 'ting-a-ling-a-ling!'?
YOU: . . . . . . . . .
KATE: A spider on a bicycle!

## Project

Are there too many people in the world? Complete the chart for this year.

| WORLD POPULATION IN MILLIONS | | | |
|---|---|---|---|
| **COUNTRY** | **1960** | **1981** | **THIS YEAR** |
| CHINA | 668 | 1,029 | |
| INDIA | 435 | 750 | |
| EUROPE | 425 | 490 | |
| USSR | 214 | 275 | |
| USA | 181 | 236 | |
| BRAZIL | 73 | 133 | |
| YOUR COUNTRY | | | |

## Joke time!

CUSTOMER: Waiter! Waiter! There are six spiders in my soup.
WAITER: I know. It's their bath night!

## Guessing game

There is a horrible spider somewhere in the room. Think of a place and write it down. The others must guess where it is.

Is it in the chimney?
Is it on the wall?

## Grammar Lessons 21-25

| How many children are there? | There are forty-five. |
|---|---|

| Is | there | a desk | in your room? |
|---|---|---|---|
| Are | | any chairs | |

| Yes, | there | is. |
|---|---|---|
| No, | | isn't. |
| Yes, | | are. |
| No, | | aren't. |

| There | 's | an | old | castle in my town. | |
|---|---|---|---|---|---|
| | are | some many | beautiful interesting | gardens things to see | in Dover. |
| | aren't any | | | | |

| Where's the box? | It's | in under on next to near | the bed. |
|---|---|---|---|

| Where's (*name of place*)? | It's | in the | north south east west centre | of Britain. |
|---|---|---|---|---|

| It's on the | north south east west | coast of Britain. |
|---|---|---|

| I live He/she lives | in | Dover. the centre of Belfast. the north of England. |
|---|---|---|

| Why is Dover important? | Because it's a link between Britain and Europe. |
|---|---|

| *Possessive adjective* its | *Possessive pronouns* ours theirs | *Genitive plural* my parents' room |
|---|---|---|

# How do you spell it?

### ▣ Dialogue

| | |
|---|---|
| MAN: | T-shirts and posters with your name on! |
| SUE: | Come and have a look Kate. |
| MAN: | Do you want a T-shirt or a poster? |
| SUE: | Can I have a T-shirt, please? |
| MAN: | OK. What's your name? |
| SUE: | Sue Wilson. |
| MAN: | How do you spell your surname? |
| SUE: | W-I-L-S-O-N. |
| MAN: | Do you want anything else on it? |
| SUE: | Yes. I want 'Sue Wilson is great, OK?' |

**The alphabet**
There are twenty-six letters in the English alphabet:

ABCDEFGHIJKLMNOPQRSTUVWXYZ
a b c d e f g h i j k l m n o p q r s t u v w x y z

There are five vowels:

A E I O U

and twenty-one consonants:

B C D F G H J K L M N P Q R S T V W X Y Z

**1** ▣ **Listen and repeat.**

**2** **Ask and answer about names.**

| | |
|---|---|
| YOU: | What's your surname? |
| FRIEND: | Harrison. |
| YOU: | How do you spell it? |
| FRIEND: | H-A- double R-I-S-O-N. |

**3** **Spelling quiz**

How do you spell it in English?

1. The name of your country
2. The name of your capital city
3. The name of your school
4. The name of your headmaster or headmistress
5. The capital of France
6. The capital of Brazil
7. The capital of Japan
8. The president of the United States

**4** It is your birthday. Look at the pictures below and say what you want.

FRIEND: Do you want a torch or a bicycle lamp?
YOU: Can I have a torch, please?

*a torch*

*a bicycle lamp* *a record* *a cassette*

*a wallet* *a purse* *a pair of scissors* *a penknife*

*a comb* *a brush* *some jeans* *some trainers*

**Joke time!**

Mississippi is a big word. How do you spell it?

M.I.S.S...

No, you're wrong. The answer is 'I.T.'

### THE CHAMPIONS

# Can you run fast?
# Can you climb a rope?
# Can you swim under water?

You can? That's terrific!
Do you want to be a member of the Dover Team for
The Champions Competition?

You do? That's great!
Please send your name, address, age,
the name of your school and the name of your sports teacher to:
The Champions Competition, Room 6, The Town Hall, Dover.

**1** Look at the chart and answer the questions about you. Write Yes, No, or Not very well .

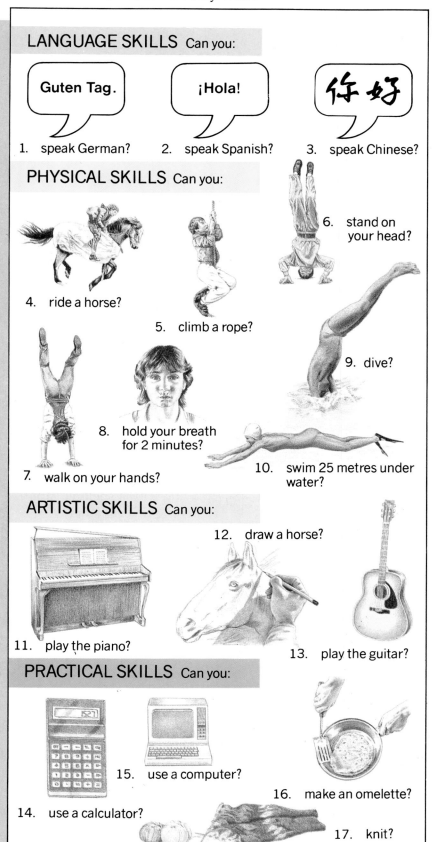

LANGUAGE SKILLS Can you:

Guten Tag.

¡Hola!

你好

1. speak German?
2. speak Spanish?
3. speak Chinese?

PHYSICAL SKILLS Can you:

6. stand on your head?

4. ride a horse?

5. climb a rope?

9. dive?

8. hold your breath for 2 minutes?

10. swim 25 metres under water?

7. walk on your hands?

ARTISTIC SKILLS Can you:

12. draw a horse?

11. play the piano?

13. play the guitar?

PRACTICAL SKILLS Can you:

15. use a computer?

16. make an omelette?

14. use a calculator?

17. knit?

**2** Work in pairs. Ask and answer the questions and write Yes, No or Not very well **for your friend.**

YOU: Can you speak German?
FRIEND: Yes, I can but not very well. Can you?
YOU: No, I can't.

*Look!*
can't = cannot

**3** Tell your teacher what your friend can and cannot do.

Marianne can speak German but she can't speak English very well.

**4** From each section of the chart, write sentences about some of the things you can do and some of the things you cannot do.

I can play the piano but I can't play the guitar.

**Did you know?**

Llamas can move their ears one at a time or both together.

# I'm doing my homework.

## 📼 Dialogue

LUCY: What are you doing?
ANDY: Go away. I'm doing my homework.
LUCY: No, you aren't. You're writing a letter.
ANDY: No, I'm not.
LUCY: Yes, you are! You're writing to Amanda. Is she your girlfriend?
ANDY: Be quiet and mind your own business!
LUCY: Andy's got a girlfriend! Andy's got a girlfriend!

**1** Ask the people in the pictures below what they're doing. Imagine you are the people.

YOU: What are you doing, Andy?
FRIEND: I'm writing a letter.

1. *writing a letter*

2. *playing with a spelling game*

3. *listening to the radio*

4. *watching TV*

5. *talking to a friend on the telephone*

6. *making some toffee*

**2** Talk to the people in the pictures again.

YOU: Are you writing a postcard, Andy?
FRIEND: No, I'm not. I'm writing a letter.
YOU: Are you playing with a spelling game, Lucy?
FRIEND: Yes, I am.

1. Andy — writing a postcard?
2. Lucy — playing with a spelling game?
3. Kate — listening to a cassette?
4. Mrs Morgan — watching TV?
5. Mr Morgan — talking to your mother?
6. John — making some hot chocolate?

**3** Mime an action (swimming, walking, etc) and see if your friends can guess what you're doing.

> *Look!*
>
> | do | do**ing** | write | writ**ing** |
> |---|---|---|---|
> | talk | talk**ing** | make | mak**ing** |

# She's wearing Number 13.

1. Alan Wells
   200 metres

2. Poland v Italy
   football

3. Brazil v Yugoslavia  volleyball

4. Marita Koch
   200 metres

5. Michael Gross
   100 metres butterfly

**1** **Ask and say what the people in the pictures above are doing.**

YOU:  What is he doing in picture 1?
FRIEND:  He's running.

YOU:  What are they doing in picture 2?
FRIEND:  They're playing football.

**2** **Correct the statements about the pictures above.**

1. He's running in the 800 metres.
   He isn't running in the 800 metres, he's running in the 200 metres.
2. They're playing basketball.
   They aren't playing basketball, they're playing football.

1. He's running in the 800 metres.
2. They're playing basketball.
3. Brazil are playing Germany.
4. She's running in the Marathon.
5. He's diving.

## 🔊 Dialogue

JOHN:  I can see Tracy. She's wearing Number 13.
SUE:  That's unlucky.
JOHN:  She's standing next to Mrs Todd.
SUE:  That's unlucky, too!
JOHN:  What are Tracy and Simon doing? I don't understand.
SUE:  They're tying a scarf round their ankles. It's the three-legged race!
MAN:  On your marks, get set, go!
JOHN:  Can you see them? Are they first?
SUE:  No, they aren't. They're third.
JOHN:  Sit down, Sue. I can't see!
SUE:  No. You stand up instead. Look, they're second now.
KATE:  Come on Dover!

Look!
first
second
third
last

## Listen and read

**Correct these statements.**

1. Nicola and Jack are at school.
   No, they aren't. They're on holiday.

1. Nicola and Jack are at school.
2. They are swimming on Puffin Island.
3. The men are wearing sweaters and jeans.
4. The men are rowing to the beach.
5. Jack and Nicola are having a cup of tea.
6. Jack and Nicola are fishing on the island.

## 🎧 Conversation

Complete the conversation with Andy.

ANDY: How do you spell your surname?

YOU: . . . . . . . . .

ANDY: OK. What sports and games are you doing at school now?

YOU: . . . . . . . . .

ANDY: What languages are you learning?

YOU: . . . . . . . . .

ANDY: Can you speak French?

YOU: . . . . . . . . .

ANDY: I can speak a little but not very well. I must go now. Bye!

YOU: . . . . . . . . .

## Write

Look again at the picture story and write sentences to say what is happening in the pictures.

Nicola and Jack are watching . . .

### Did you know?

The giant tortoises of the Galapagos Islands can live over 150 years.

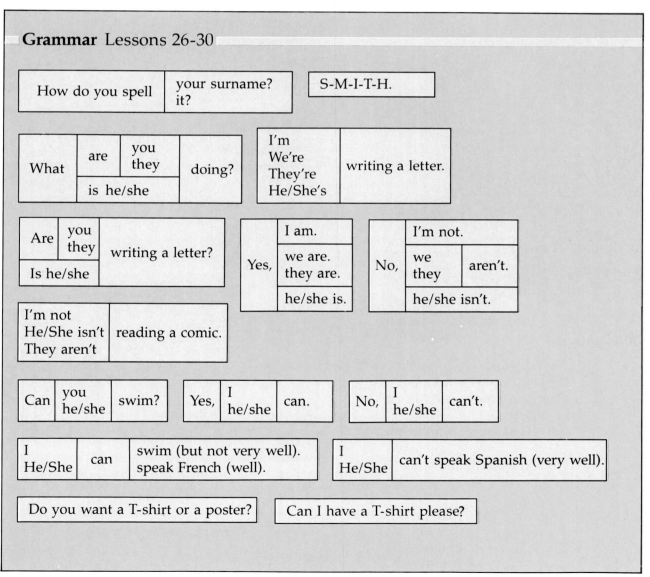

## Grammar Lessons 26-30

| How do you spell | your surname? it? | S-M-I-T-H. |

| What | are | you they | doing? |
|      | is he/she | | |

| I'm / We're / They're / He/She's | writing a letter. |

| Are | you they | writing a letter? |
| Is he/she | | |

| Yes, | I am. / we are. they are. / he/she is. |

| No, | I'm not. / we they aren't. / he/she isn't. |

| I'm not / He/She isn't / They aren't | reading a comic. |

| Can | you he/she | swim? |

| Yes, | I he/she | can. |

| No, | I he/she | can't. |

| I / He/She | can | swim (but not very well). speak French (well). |

| I / He/She | can't speak Spanish (very well). |

| Do you want a T-shirt or a poster? | Can I have a T-shirt please? |

# Do you like hamburgers?

WELCOME TO WIMPY

**Hamburger** 64p
100% beef patty, served with ketchup and diced onion in a freshly toasted, white, sesame seeded bun.

**Cheeseburger** 74p
A tasty slice of melted cheese tops our 100% beef patty, with ketchup, diced onion and a sesame seeded bun.

**Wimpy Kingsize** £1.26
Two 100% beef patties with melted cheese between them, topped with ketchup and dressed with lettuce, tomato and diced onion, all in a white sesame seeded bun.

*Brown Buns*

**Quarterpounder*** £1.21
A delicious ¼ pound of beef in a large brown bun, dressed with lettuce, diced onion and our tangy Special Sauce.

**Quarterpounder*** with Cheese £1.31
Our delicious Quarterpounder with the extra flavour of a slice of melted cheese.

*Brown Bun*

**Halfpounder*** with Cheese £1.99
A mighty meal – a full ½ pound of juicy beef in a large brown bun, dressed with lettuce, diced onion, melted cheese and our own tangy Special Sauce.

**Fish and Chips** £1.44
A succulent fish portion fried in golden breadcrumbs, served with chips and sachets of salt and vinegar.

VAT is excluded on some take-away items.

*Approx. uncooked weight

Our Guarantee
Wimpy hamburger patties are made entirely from 100% beef with spices.

**Chicken in a Bun** £1.2
Tender white chicken covered with a thin crispy batter, dressed with lettuce and a creamy sauce in a white sesame seeded bun.

**Chips** 55p
Golden and crisp – the way you love them

**Sparkling Orange** or PEPSI 45p / 50p

**Hot Apple Pie** 50p

**Pure Orange Juice** 58p

**Thick Milk Shakes** Strawberry, Chocolate, Banana
TAKE AWAY 58p EAT IN 65p

**Coffee** 45p **Hot Chocolate** 45p

**Tea** 38p **Toasted Tea Cake** 40p

BREAKFAST SPECIAL

**Bacon and Egg in a Bun** 92p
Two rashers of prime back bacon and a fried egg, topped with ketchup and served in a white sesame seeded bun.

**Bacon in a Bun** 77p
Two rashers of prime back bacon topped with ketchup and served in a white sesame seeded bun.
Served until 11am

START YOUR DAY THE WIMPY WAY

© Wimpy International Ltd 1985    * Wimpy is a registered trademark.

## 📼 Dialogue

MAN: Next, please.

MR MORGAN: What do you want, Kate?

KATE: Can I have a cheeseburger and chips, please?

MR MORGAN: Two cheeseburgers and chips, please.

MAN: Do you want them with or without onions?

KATE: Without.

MR MORGAN: She doesn't like onions.

MAN: Do you want mustard?

KATE: No thanks. I don't like mustard, either. Just ketchup, please.

**1** Look at the menu and find:

a cheeseburger     a milkshake
a hamburger        a cup of coffee
chips              an orange juice
apple pie          a Pepsi Cola

FOOD

*tomato soup*

*fish and chips*

*chicken*

*apple pie*

THINGS TO GO WITH FOOD

*salt and pepper*      *mustard*      *tomato ketchup*      *onions*

DRINKS

*coffee*      *milk*      *tea*      *Coca-Cola*

*orange juice*      *chocolate milkshake*      *banana milkshake*      *strawberry milkshake*

**2** **Ask and answer.**

YOU:  Do you like tomato soup?
FRIEND:  Yes, I do.
YOU:  Do you like fish and chips?
FRIEND:  No, I don't.

**3** **Write down all the things you like and all the things you don't like. Write two lists:** I like ... I don't like ...

**4** **Change lists with your partner and write two things your partner likes and two things your partner doesn't like.**

Maria likes hamburgers and chips but she doesn't like tomato ketchup or onions.

**Did you know?**

The biggest hamburger ever made was in Perth, Australia in 1976. It weighed 1,297 kilograms and measured 8.38 metres round!

# Which ones do you like?

## 🔊 Dialogue

MR MORGAN: Which trainers do you like?
Do you like those?
KATE: Which ones?
MR MORGAN: The grey ones.
KATE: No, I don't. I like the pink ones.
They're really nice.
WOMAN: Can I help you?
KATE: No, thanks. We're just looking at trainers.
WOMAN: Fine. Our new trainers are in the window.

### 1 Choose and point to the ones you like.

YOU: Which sports bag do you like?
FRIEND: I like that/this one.
YOU: Which trainers do you like?
FRIEND: I like these/those.

1. sports bags          2. trainers

3. shorts          4. sweaters

5. T-shirts          6. anoraks

7. track suits          8. roller skates

### 2 Say what you like.

YOU: I like the red and silver sports bag.
FRIEND: I don't. I like the green one./Yes, I like it too. It's really nice.

YOU: I like the blue trainers.
FRIEND: I don't. I like the red ones./Yes, I like them too. They're really nice.

### 3 Ask and answer.

YOU: Do you like these/those shorts?
FRIEND: Which ones?
YOU: The white ones.
FRIEND: Yes, I do./No, I don't.

### 4 Look at the items in exercise 1 again and write five sentences about the things you like and don't like.

I like the blue trainers but I don't like the red ones.

### 5 Write down two things your partner likes and two things your partner doesn't like.

Tony likes the green sports bag but he doesn't like the red and silver one. He likes....

# When have we got Maths?

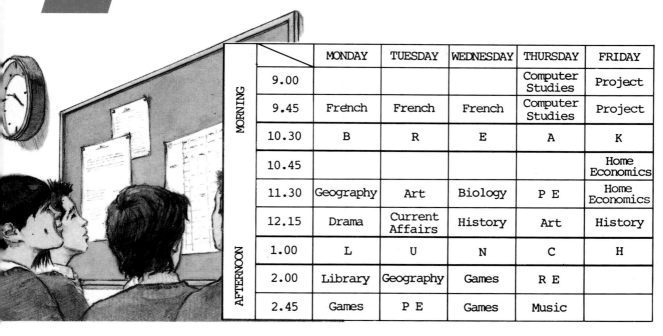

| | | MONDAY | TUESDAY | WEDNESDAY | THURSDAY | FRIDAY |
|---|---|---|---|---|---|---|
| MORNING | 9.00 | | | | Computer Studies | Project |
| | 9.45 | French | French | French | Computer Studies | Project |
| | 10.30 | B | R | E | A | K |
| | 10.45 | | | | | Home Economics |
| | 11.30 | Geography | Art | Biology | P E | Home Economics |
| | 12.15 | Drama | Current Affairs | History | Art | History |
| AFTERNOON | 1.00 | L | U | N | C | H |
| | 2.00 | Library | Geography | Games | R E | |
| | 2.45 | Games | P E | Games | Music | |

## 🔊 Dialogue

ANDY: Oh no! We've got English on Monday, Tuesday and Wednesday morning.
JOHN: When have we got Maths?
ANDY: Every day except Friday. And look! We've got double Science with Mr Bragg.
JOHN: When?
ANDY: On Friday afternoon.
JOHN: How horrible!

**1** Read the dialogue and complete the timetable above.

**2** On which day or days is:

1. Biology?
   It's on Wednesday.

1. Biology?
2. History?
3. Computer Studies?
4. French?
5. Games?
6. Home Economics?

**3** Ask and say exactly when the lessons are.

YOU: When is Biology?
FRIEND: It's on Wednesday morning.

**4** Talk about your timetable.

YOU: When have we got Games?
FRIEND: On Monday and Wednesday afternoon.

**5** Ask and answer.

YOU: What are your best subjects?
FRIEND: My best subjects are Maths and Science. What are yours?

**6** 🔊 Listen, and repeat.

The days of the week:
Monday     Friday
Tuesday    Saturday ⎫
Wednesday  Sunday   ⎬ the weekend
Thursday            ⎭

🔊 Rhyme

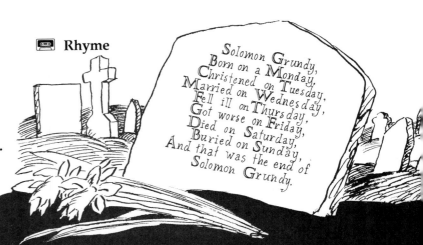

Solomon Grundy,
Born on a Monday,
Christened on Tuesday,
Married on Wednesday,
Fell ill on Thursday,
Got worse on Friday,
Died on Saturday,
Buried on Sunday,
And that was the end of
Solomon Grundy.

# Do you like swimming?

**CAMP SHERWOOD**

M O R E   T H A N   J U S T   A   H O L I D A Y

What do you like doing in your free time? Do you like swimming, riding and sailing? You do? Then come and join us here at Camp Sherwood. It's the perfect place for an adventure holiday.

Look at the questionnaire. Tick the things that you like doing and put a star by the activities that you can do well. Send the form to Barry Smith at the following address: Camp Sherwood, PO Box 12, Taunton, Somerset

**Outdoor activities**

Do you like:
horse riding?
riding BMX bikes?
climbing?
birdwatching?
playing tennis?
playing football?

---

**1** Look at the brochure above. Write down your two favourite activities from each group. Then write a sentence about each activity.

I like playing tennis very much.

**2** Write down an activity from each group that you don't like doing very much. Then write a sentence about each activity.

I don't like playing football very much.

*Look!*

So do I.    Neither do I.
So can I.    Neither can I.

**3** Talk about the things you like or don't like doing.

YOU:      Do you like climbing?
FRIEND:  Yes, I do.
YOU:      So do I.

YOU:      Do you like playing football?
FRIEND:  No, I don't.
YOU:      Neither do I.

53 (fifty-three)

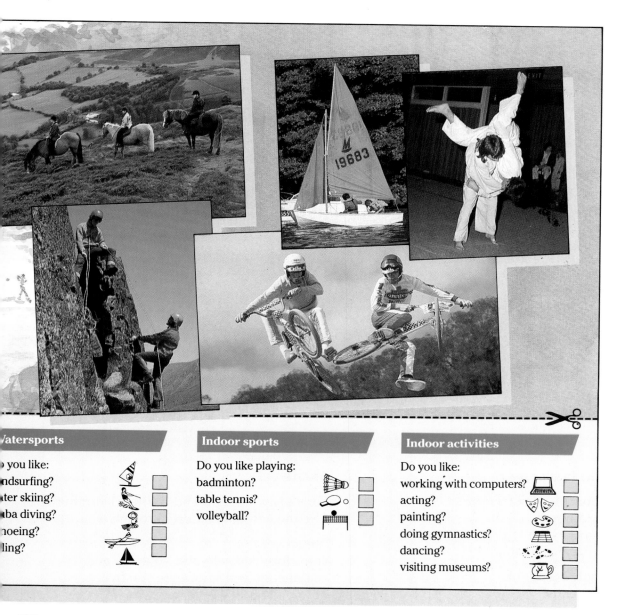

| Watersports | | Indoor sports | | Indoor activities | |
|---|---|---|---|---|---|
| Do you like: | | Do you like playing: | | Do you like: | |
| windsurfing? | ☐ | badminton? | ☐ | working with computers? | ☐ |
| water skiing? | ☐ | table tennis? | ☐ | acting? | ☐ |
| scuba diving? | ☐ | volleyball? | ☐ | painting? | ☐ |
| canoeing? | ☐ | | | doing gymnastics? | ☐ |
| sailing? | ☐ | | | dancing? | ☐ |
| | | | | visiting museums? | ☐ |

**4** **Talk about the things you can or can't do.**

YOU: Can you windsurf?
FRIEND: Yes, I can.
YOU: So can I.

YOU: Can you water ski?
FRIEND: No, I can't.
YOU: Neither can I.

**5** **Choose two members of your family and write what each of them likes and doesn't like doing.**

My brother George likes ... but he doesn't like .... My mother ...

**Joke time!**

CUSTOMER: Waiter! Waiter! I don't like this cheese.
WAITER: Why don't you like it, sir?
CUSTOMER: There are holes in it.
WAITER: Well, eat the cheese and leave the holes on your plate.

## Read

# TARETA · LIVES · ON · AN · ISLAND

THE COOK ISLANDS

Aitutaki

Rarotonga

Tareta Riki is thirteen years old. She is Polynesian and lives on the little island of Aitutaki in the south of the central Pacific Ocean. Aitutaki is one of a group of islands called the Cook Islands.

Tareta has two sisters and a brother. Her mother is a customs officer at the airport and her father is an ambulance driver at the island hospital. Her elder brother doesn't live at home. He is married and lives in New Zealand.

Tareta goes to school on the island. 'I like most subjects. I like learning new things. My favourite subject is physics but I also like gymnastics and volleyball. We have homework to do every evening.

At home in the evenings I like cooking and making clothes. At the weekend, on Saturday, I have dancing classes. I love dancing and listening to music.'

### Which is the best answer?

1. Paragraph 1 is about Tareta's:
   a) island home.
   b) family.
   c) the Pacific Ocean.

2. Paragraph 2 is about:
   a) her friends.
   b) her job.
   c) her family.

3. Paragraph 3 is mainly about:
   a) sport.
   b) her school subjects.
   c) her free time activities.

4. Paragraph 4 is about:
   a) her free time activities.
   b) her homework.
   c) Saturday and Sunday.

## Write

Tareta is your penfriend. Write a letter to her. Use the letter in Lesson 24 to help you.

*Paragraph 1*
Introduce yourself: give your age and nationality, and say where you live.

*Paragraph 2*
Tell Tareta about your family: say who they are and what their jobs are.

*Paragraph 3*
Tell Tareta about your school and your favourite school subjects. Say which days of the week they are on.

*Paragraph 4*
Tell her about your favourite sports and activities. Also say what you like doing in the evenings.

### Finish your letter with

*Looking forward to hearing from you.*
              *Best wishes,*

## 🔊 Conversation

Complete the conversation with Andy.

ANDY: We've got Maths every day except
Friday. What about you?

YOU: .........

ANDY: When have you got Games?

YOU: .........

ANDY: What sports do you like?

YOU: .........

ANDY: There's a super new hamburger bar
near our school. Do you like hamburgers?

YOU: .........

ANDY: I like chocolate milkshakes. Which
flavour do you like?

YOU: .........

ANDY: Anyway, I must go. It's time for my
music lesson. Bye. See you!

YOU: .........

## 🔊 Listen

Listen to Melanie talking about her school
subjects and on which days she has them.
Copy the chart and make notes to complete it.

| Name | Age | Favourite subjects | Days |
|------|-----|--------------------|------|
|      |     |                    |      |
|      |     |                    |      |

## Project

In your class, what are the three most popular:

school subjects?   outdoor sports?
indoor activities?

## Grammar Lessons 31-35

| Do you like | hamburgers?<br>swimming?<br>these/those shorts? |
|---|---|

| Yes, | I | do. |
|---|---|---|
| No, | | don't. |

| Do you want | mustard?<br>onions? |
|---|---|

| Which | sports bag<br>one<br>trainers<br>ones | do you like? |
|---|---|---|

| I like | this/that<br>the red | one. |
|---|---|---|
| | these /those.<br>the red ones. | |

| I like | cheeseburgers.<br>tea.<br>swimming. |
|---|---|
| He/She likes | |

So do I.

| I don't | like | mustard.<br>playing tennis. |
|---|---|---|
| He/She doesn't | | |

Neither do I.

I can swim.   So can I.   I can't skate.   Neither can I.

When have we got Maths?

| We've got Maths on | Monday. | |
|---|---|---|
| | Tuesday | morning.<br>afternoon. |

Have we got Maths on Friday?

| Yes, | we | have. |
|---|---|---|
| No, | | haven't. |

### My Pets

We have got three family pets: a dog, a cat and a tortoise. The dog's name is Big Ben. He is a big golden Labrador. He is beautiful. He has got big brown eyes and a long tail. He is a very friendly dog but he is sometimes a bit stupid. Dogs are expensive to keep but they are very good guards for the house.

Our cat is called Cleopatra. She is quite young but she is not a kitten. She is very pretty. She has got black and white fur and green eyes. She's clever, too, and very clean.

The tortoise's name is Rocky. He has got short, fat legs, a long neck and a very hard shell. He is also very old and slow. He's ugly and dirty but I like him.

**1** Read Kate's composition. Answer about the pets.

**Answer about Big Ben.**

1. Is Big Ben small?
   No, he isn't. He's big.

1. Is Big Ben small?
2. What sort of dog is he?
3. Is he ugly?
4. What colour are his eyes?
5. Is his tail short?
6. Is he unfriendly?
7. Is he a clever dog?
8. Are dogs cheap pets?

**Answer about Cleopatra.**

1. Is she a kitten?
2. Is she ugly?
3. Is she dirty?

**Answer about Rocky.**

1. What sort of animal is Rocky?
2. Are Rocky's legs long and thin?
3. Is his shell soft?
4. Is he young?

1. GIRAFFE (AFRICA)

2. SPIDER MONKEY (SOUTH AMERICA)

3. KOALA BEAR (AUSTRALIA)

4. ANTEATER (SOUTH AMERICA)

5. GIANT CRAB (ASIA)

6. LEOPARD (AFRICA)

7. ZEBRA (AFRICA)

**2** **In pairs, find an animal with one of the following:**

a long tongue  long arms
a small nose  soft fur
a hard shell  thin legs
a short tail  small spots
a long neck  big spots
small ears  black and white stripes

**3** **Talk about the animals.**

YOU: What's special about a giraffe?

FRIEND: It's got a very long neck, long thin legs and small ears.

**4** **Write about the animals.**

1. This is a giraffe. It has long thin legs, a very long neck and small ears. It lives in Africa.

**5** **Guess the animal.**

One person thinks of an animal. The other person must ask questions to guess which animal it is.

YOU: What's it like?

FRIEND: It's black and white. It's got big spots and small ears and it lives in China.

YOU: I know! It's a panda.

# It's too high!

## 🔊 Dialogue

LUCY: Look! That nasty dog from next door is chasing Cleo!

ANDY: Cleo's in the tree. She can't get down. Be quiet, you noisy dog!

JOHN: It's no good. I can't reach her. It's too dangerous. Help!

ANDY: What's the matter?

JOHN: I'm frightened! I'm slipping!

ANDY: Hang on to the branch and move along it. It's easy! It's quite safe!

JOHN: No, I'm too heavy.

ANDY: Let go and drop.

JOHN: It's too high!

ANDY: Help! Help! Someone bring a ladder!

### 1 True or False?

1. The dog next door is a nice dog.
2. The dog is chasing the cat.
3. The cat can't get down.
4. The cat is slipping.
5. Andy and John are in the tree.
6. John can reach the cat.
7. The branch is low.

### 2 Look at the pictures below and ask and say what the matter is.

1. YOU: What's the matter?
   FRIEND: It's too difficult.
2. YOU: What's the matter?
   FRIEND: It's too hot.

### Choose from this list:
heavy easy hot small long noisy cold big short difficult high dangerous low light

### 3 Write sentences to say what you think of:

1. your school day
   Our school day is too long.

1. your school day
2. your school holidays
3. your exams
4. your village/town/capital city

### Joke time!

Tell me about your exam questions.

The questions are very easy. But the answers are too difficult!

# Speak loudly and clearly!

## 🔊 Dialogue

| | |
|---|---|
| KATE: | Dad, I need some help with my French speech. |
| MR MORGAN: | OK. Go on. |
| KATE: | 'Bonjour…' Wait a moment! The TV's too loud. |
| MR MORGAN: | Turn it off. It isn't very interesting. |
| KATE: | 'Bonjour…' |
| MR MORGAN: | No, you're speaking too quietly. I can't hear you. Speak loudly. |
| KATE: | 'Bonjour, Mesdames et Messieurs, je suis…' |
| MR MORGAN: | Stop! Now you're speaking too fast! Speak slowly and clearly. |
| KATE: | 'Bon-jour, Mes-dam-es et Mes-sieurs je-…' |
| MR MORGAN: | That's too slow now. |
| KATE: | OK. What about this? 'Good evening Ladies and Gentlemen. I am very happy to welcome you to our school in Dover.' |
| MR MORGAN: | That's very nice! |
| KATE: | Oh Dad! |

**1** Complete these sentences with words from the dialogue.

1. The television is too ….
2. The television programme is not very ….
3. At first Kate speaks too … so her father asks her to speak ….
4. Then she speaks too … so her father asks her to speak … and ….
5. Then Kate speaks too ….
6. At last her father says her speech is ….

**2** Look at the pictures below. In pairs, ask and answer the questions correctly.

YOU:    Are they running slowly?
FRIEND:  No, they're running fast.

1   Are they running slowly?
2.  Are they smiling nastily?
3.  Are they walking fast?
4.  Are they singing quietly?
5.  Is he talking loudly?
6.  Is he walking slowly?

**3** Ask different people in the class to do these things.

1. Go to the front of the class slowly.
2. Say *good morning* loudly.
3. Walk towards the door quickly.
4. Shut the door quietly.
5. Go back to your seat slowly.
6. Say your name and address slowly and clearly.
7. Say *thank you* nicely.
8. You are Dracula. Say *Come here my little friend* nastily.

**Joke time!**

How do Eskimos get dressed?

Very quickly!

# How tall is it?

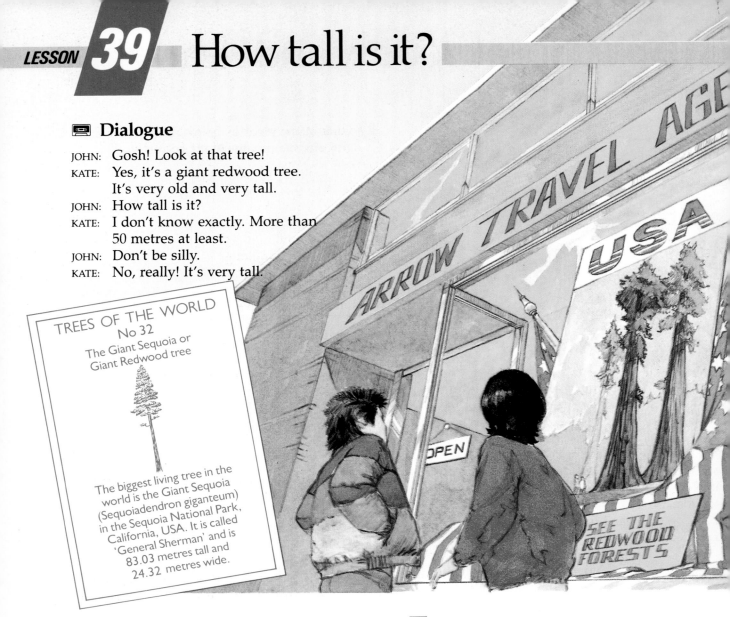

## 📼 Dialogue

JOHN: Gosh! Look at that tree!
KATE: Yes, it's a giant redwood tree.
 It's very old and very tall.
JOHN: How tall is it?
KATE: I don't know exactly. More than
 50 metres at least.
JOHN: Don't be silly.
KATE: No, really! It's very tall.

TREES OF THE WORLD
No 32
The Giant Sequoia or
Giant Redwood tree

The biggest living tree in the
world is the Giant Sequoia
(Sequoiadendron giganteum)
in the Sequoia National Park,
California, USA. It is called
'General Sherman' and is
83.03 metres tall and
24.32 metres wide.

### 1 Answer the questions.

1. Why are redwood trees special?
2. Where can you see them?
3. How tall is General Sherman?
4. How wide is it?

*Look!*

| | |
|---|---|
| mm = millimetre | in = inch |
| cm = centimere | ft = foot/feet |
| m = metre | yd = yard |
| km = kilometre | mile |

### 2 Height

YOU: How tall/high is General Sherman?
FRIEND: It's 83.03 metres tall/high.

**Ask and answer about the height of famous landmarks.**

1. *The Eiffel Tower (300.5 m)*
2. *The Great Pyramid of Giza (146.58 m)*
3. *The World Trade Center (412.4 m)*

**Ask and answer about your height.**

YOU: How tall are you?
FRIEND: I'm 1 metre 43 centimetres tall.

## 3 Length

YOU: How long is the Golden Gate Bridge in San Francisco?

FRIEND: It's 1,260 metres long.

**Ask and answer about the length of the boats.**

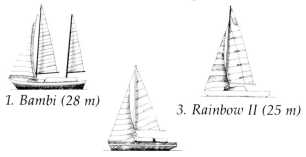

1. *Bambi (28 m)*

3. *Rainbow II (25 m)*

2. *Freestyle (30 m)*

## 4 Width and depth

YOU: How wide are the Niagara Falls?

FRIEND: They're 750 metres wide.

YOU: How deep is the Pacific Ocean?

FRIEND: It's ... Oh, I don't know!

**Ask about the measurements of the swimming pool.**

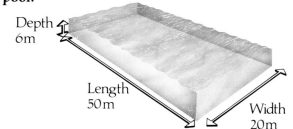

Depth 6m

Length 50m

Width 20m

## 5 Distance

YOU: How far is it from London to New York?

FRIEND: It's 5,565 kilometres.

**You are in Calais. Ask about the distances to different places in Europe.**

| Paris | 314 km |
|---|---|
| Dover | 41 km |
| London | 166 km |
| Ostend | 90 km |

## 6 Quiz

1. How high is Mount Everest?
   Is it a) 8,700 m high?
   b) 4,410 m high?
   c) 5,802 m high?
2. How long is the Amazon River?
   Is it a) 7,100 km long?
   b) 6,300 km long?
   c) 4,400 km long?
3. How far is it from the earth to the moon?
   Is it a) nearly a million kilometres?
   b) nearly half a million kilometres?
   c) nearly a quarter of a million kilometres?
4. How wide is the Grand Canyon?
   Is it a) 29 km wide?
   b) 72 km wide?
   c) 10 km wide?

## 7 Write about one of the following in your country:

a mountain
a river
a famous building

**Give its name and any other interesting facts you know about it. Say how far it is from your home.**

## 8 Measure:

the width of your finger.
the length of your little finger.
the height of your friend.
the distance from your desk to the window.

## 9 Find out the following information about a swimming pool in your area:

length
width
depth at the deep end and shallow end

**Read**

# REAL LIFE OR *FANTASY*

Do you like American 'soap operas'?  They are called 'real life' stories, but how real are they?

Millions of people all over the world love watching American TV programmes like *Dallas* and *Dynasty*. The names of some of their characters like J.R. and Sue Ellen in *Dallas*, and Alexis and Blake Carrington in *Dynasty* are well known in many countries.

Why are these programmes so popular? Perhaps it's because they are not like real life at all. Nothing is ever ugly or old-fashioned. The women are either young and beautiful or old and beautiful. The men are either clever and good-looking or stupid and good-looking. The people are never fat.

The families are always very rich. They live in very large houses, they drive fast cars and they wear expensive clothes. Nothing in Dallas or Denver is cheap!

DYNASTY

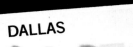

DALLAS

### Answer the questions.

How does the article describe:
the women in soap operas?
the men?
the families?
the houses?
the cars?
the clothes?

### Write

Write some sentences to explain why American soap operas are not like real life. Write a sentence about each of the topics above. Use *too* with an adjective in each sentence. **Begin:**
The women are too beautiful.

## 📼 Conversation

Complete the conversation with Kate. You are talking on the telephone.

KATE:  Hello. It's me again. Tell me, where do you live?

YOU:  . . . . . . . . .

KATE:  Wait a moment! I can't hear. Say it again loudly and clearly.

YOU:  . . . . . . . . .

KATE:  OK. Thanks. Is it a big place?

YOU:  . . . . . . . . .

KATE:  What's your school like?

YOU:  . . . . . . . . .

KATE:  Are you a noisy class?

YOU:  . . . . . . . . .

KATE:  Do you think English is easy?

YOU:  . . . . . . . . .

KATE:  Anyway, I must go. Bye!

YOU:  . . . . . . . . .

## 📼 Listen

Sue, John and Andy are rehearsing for the school play. The drama teacher is helping them. Match the teacher's comments with the correct person.

| ANDY. . . | is speaking too fast. |
|---|---|
| JOHN. . . | is not speaking clearly. |
| SUE. . . | is speaking too quietly and too slowly. |

**Joke time!**

What's big, hairy and flies at 2,000mph?

King Kongcorde.

## Grammar Lessons 36-40

| Is he/she tall? | Are they friendly? | What's it like? |
|---|---|---|

| It's too | high.<br>difficult. | | It's | very<br>not very<br>quite | easy. | | It's got/It has | a long nose.<br>very short ears. |
|---|---|---|---|---|---|---|---|---|

| He/She is walking | too<br>very | quickly. | | Open<br>Walk to | the door | slowly.<br>quietly. |
|---|---|---|---|---|---|---|

| How far is it from New York to London? | It's 5,565 km. |
|---|---|

| How tall | are you? | | I'm<br>He's | 1 m 50 cm | tall. |
|---|---|---|---|---|---|
| | is | Andy?<br>it? | It's 200 m | | |

| How | high | is | General Sherman? | It's | 83.03 m (high). |
|---|---|---|---|---|---|
| | long | | the River Amazon? | | 4,132 miles (long). |
| | wide | | your desk? | | 320 cm (wide). |
| | deep | | the swimming pool? | | 7 m (deep). |

*Adjectives:* quiet nice nasty fast
*Adverbs:* quietly nicely nastily fast

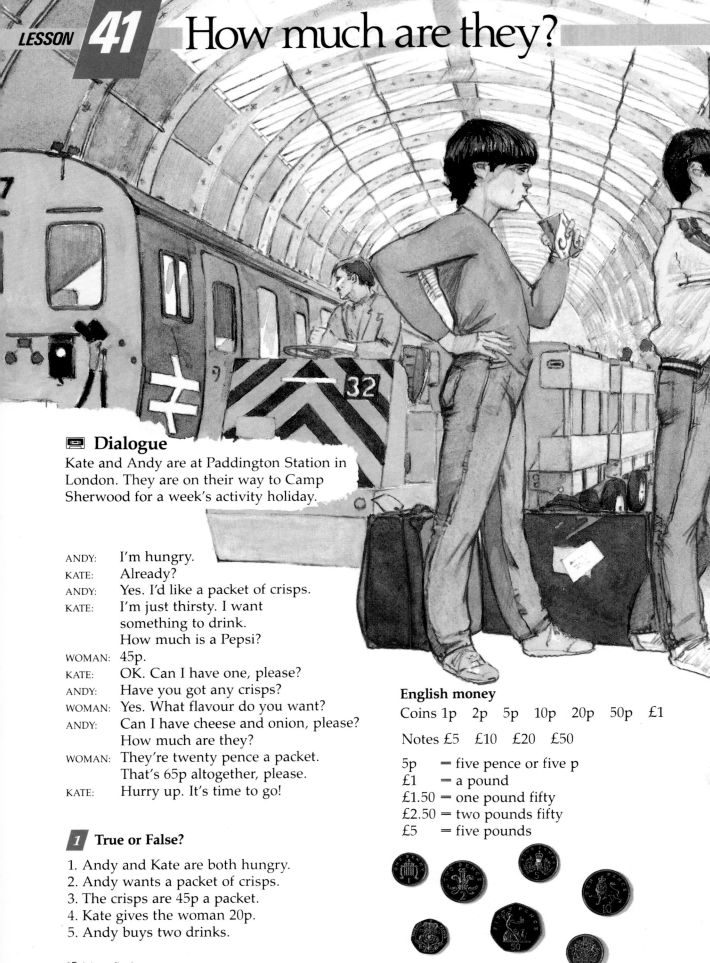

# How much are they?

## 🔲 Dialogue

Kate and Andy are at Paddington Station in London. They are on their way to Camp Sherwood for a week's activity holiday.

| | |
|---|---|
| ANDY: | I'm hungry. |
| KATE: | Already? |
| ANDY: | Yes. I'd like a packet of crisps. |
| KATE: | I'm just thirsty. I want something to drink. How much is a Pepsi? |
| WOMAN: | 45p. |
| KATE: | OK. Can I have one, please? |
| ANDY: | Have you got any crisps? |
| WOMAN: | Yes. What flavour do you want? |
| ANDY: | Can I have cheese and onion, please? How much are they? |
| WOMAN: | They're twenty pence a packet. That's 65p altogether, please. |
| KATE: | Hurry up. It's time to go! |

### English money

Coins 1p 2p 5p 10p 20p 50p £1

Notes £5 £10 £20 £50

5p = five pence or five p
£1 = a pound
£1.50 = one pound fifty
£2.50 = two pounds fifty
£5 = five pounds

### 1 True or False?

1. Andy and Kate are both hungry.
2. Andy wants a packet of crisps.
3. The crisps are 45p a packet.
4. Kate gives the woman 20p.
5. Andy buys two drinks.

**2** **Ask and answer about the prices of the food and drink in the pictures below.**

YOU: How much is a packet of biscuits?
FRIEND: It's 30p.
YOU: How much are the oranges?
FRIEND: They're 19p each.

*a packet of biscuits (30p)*     *a packet of crisps (20p)*     *a packet of nuts (50p)*

*oranges (19p each)*     *peaches (25p each)*     *apples (14p each)*

*Coke (45p)*     *lemonade (45p)*     *orange juice (40p)*

**3** **In pairs or groups buy things from each other.**

YOU: Have you got any biscuits?
FRIEND: Yes, I have.
YOU: How much are they?
FRIEND: They're thirty pence a packet.
YOU: Can I have two packets, please?
FRIEND: Here you are. That's 60p altogether.
YOU: Thank you.

**4** **Ask and say what you would like to eat and drink.**

YOU: I'm hungry. I'd like something to eat.
FRIEND: What do you want? I've got biscuits and crisps.
YOU: I'd like some crisps, please.

# What time is it?

## 📼 Dialogue

KATE: What time does the train arrive?
DAVE: At six o'clock. Are you tired?
KATE: No, I'm just bored. What time is it now?
DAVE: It's half past five.
KATE: Gosh, it's a long journey.
ANDY: When's supper?
DAVE: You're lucky. It's early tonight. It's at half past six. It's usually at seven o'clock.
ANDY: Hurry up, you stupid train. I'm hungry!

---

**1** Complete the sentences with the correct time.

1. The train arrives at ....
2. The time is now ....
3. Supper at Camp Sherwood tonight is at ....
4. Supper at Camp Sherwood is usually at ....

**2** Say these clock times below.

7.00
seven o'clock

7.05
five past seven

7.10
ten past seven

7.15
quarter past seven

7.20
twenty past seven

7.25
twenty-five past seven

7.30
half past seven

7.35
twenty-five to eight

7.40
twenty to eight

7.45
quarter to eight

7.50
ten to eight

7.55
five to eight

---

**3** Ask and answer about the times.

YOU: What time is it?
FRIEND: It's half past nine.

1.     2.     3.

4.     5.

**4** Use the timetable below to ask and answer about different train times.

YOU: What time does the train leave?
FRIEND: At eleven minutes past eight.
YOU: What time does the train arrive?
FRIEND: At one minute past nine.

| ⇄ **British Rail**: Windsor station and Safari park | |
| --- | --- |
| Waterloo ..... depart 8.11 | Windsor ..... arrive 9.01 |
| 8.42 | 9.30 |
| 9.12 | 10.04 |
| 9.42 | 10.30 |
| 10.12 | 11.00 |

**5** Answer the questions about you.

What time is your supper?
It's at ....
What time is your bedtime?
What time is your first lesson of the day?
What time are your English lessons?

## 📼 Dialogue

KATE: Can we go out and play volleyball?
LOUISE: No! It's raining.
ANDY: No, it isn't. The sun's shining.
Look, up there behind the clouds.
I can see the sun.
KATE: Yes, I can see it too.
LOUISE: Well, I can't. Anyway, it's Letter
Writing Hour on the timetable. OK?
Are you all writing a letter to your
parents?
CHILDREN: Yes, we are.

## The weather

*rain*     *snow*     *sun*     *cloud*

1. *It's raining.*
   *It's wet.*

2. *It's cloudy.*
   *It's dull.*

3. *It's snowing.*
   *It's cold.*
   *It's freezing.*

4. *The sun is shining.*
   *It's hot.*
   *It's warm and sunny.*

**2** Ask and say what the weather is like in each of the pictures above.

YOU: What's the weather like in picture 1?
FRIEND: It's raining./It's wet.

**3** Ask and answer more questions about the weather in the pictures.

YOU: Is it snowing/raining in picture 1?
FRIEND: No, it isn't./Yes, it is.

**1** Answer the questions.

1. What do Kate and Andy want to do?
2. What's the weather like?
3. Where's the sun?
4. What are the children doing?

**4** About your weather.

1. Ask and say what the weather's like outside at the moment.
2. On average, how many:
   centimetres of rain do you get in December?
   hours of sunshine do you get in August?

PO Box 12,
Taunton,
Somerset

CAMP SHERWOOD

Monday

Dear Mum and Dad,
How are you? The camp is OK.
The weather is horrible. It is raining. We
are all writing letters. What's the weather
like at home?
We get up every morning at a quarter to
eight and have a shower. The water is
always cold. It's really horrible!
Then we get dressed and have
breakfast at half past eight. Breakfast is
nice. We have three different sorts of
cereal, bacon and eggs, toast and marmalade
and tea.
After breakfast we go riding or canoeing.
We have a morning break at eleven o'clock.
We usually have orange juice and biscuits.
Then we have free activities.

**1** Ask and answer about
what time Kate and Andy
do things.

YOU: What time do Kate and
Andy get up?
FRIEND: They get up at a
quarter to eight.

1. get up?
2. have a shower and get
   dressed?
3. have breakfast?
4. have lunch?
5. have supper?
6. go to bed?

**2** Copy Kate and Andy's
daily diary at Camp
Sherwood. Complete it
with information from the
letter.

## DAILY DIARY

| Morning programme | | Afternoon programme | |
|---|---|---|---|
| 7.45 | We get up and | 14.30 | |
| 8.30 | | 16.00 | |
| 9.15 | | 16.30 | |
| 11.00 | | 19.00 | |
| 11.30 | We have free activities, | 19.45 | We watch a video or |
| 13.30 | | 21.30 | |

69 (sixty-nine)

We have lunch at half past one.
We have hamburgers and chips or fish
and chips but the chips aren't very nice.
In the afternoon we usually play football
or volleyball. Tea is at four o'clock and
after tea we ride on the mini motorbikes.
They're great!
 We have supper at seven. After supper
we watch a video (usually Tom and
Jerry!) or have a disco. We can play
our own cassettes. Bedtime is at half past
nine. I am in a very big room with seven
other girls. Our monitor is called Louise
but we call her Lulu.
 We're both all right and we
aren't homesick! (I am a little bit, Andy.)
 Love from Kate and Andy.

PS Please send my autograph book.

**3** **Ask and answer about Kate or Andy's routine at Camp Sherwood.**

YOU: What does Kate/Andy do after breakfast?
FRIEND: She/He goes riding or canoeing.

Ask what she/he does after breakfast.
after lunch.
after supper.

Ask what she/he has for breakfast.
for morning break.
for lunch.

**4** **Make a timetable of your own daily routine and talk about it with your partner.**

**5** **Write some sentences about your day.**

**6** **The coffee-pot game**

Think of an activity, like 'have a cold shower' and write it down. Your friends must try to guess what it is, saying the word *coffee-pot* instead of the verb. Remember they can only ask you *Yes/No* questions like:

Are you coffee-potting now?
Can Miss Harris coffee-pot?
Do you coffee-pot in the classroom?
Do you coffee-pot every day?
Do you coffee-pot in the morning?
Do you coffee-pot alone?

**Did you know?**

Hens in the USA lay about 1,380,000 eggs every minute.

## Read

### Peter and Jane in Taunton in south-west England

❝ It's spring time now. Today the weather is fine and the sun is shining. In the spring and summer we get up very early. We help our parents on the farm. At about half past seven we have a light breakfast – just orange juice, yoghurt, tea and bread and jam. We sometimes have fruit. On Saturday and Sunday we have bacon, eggs, sausages and tomatoes, with tea and toast. Breakfast is our favourite meal of the day. ❞

### Mwende in Mali in West Africa, south of the Sahara desert

❝ Here in Mali it is very hot. It is the rainy season but there is no rain. The crops are dying and everyone is hungry. In the early morning I have some millet porridge or some rice. Sometimes I have some vegetables like beans or onions. I have the same thing every day of the week. ❞

### Copy the chart and complete it with information from the texts.

|  | Peter and Jane | Mwende |
|---|---|---|
| Country |  |  |
| Weather |  |  |
| Breakfast on a weekday at the weekend |  |  |

## Project

Make a survey of your class. Find out what time people get up and go to bed. Make a graph like the one below for each question.

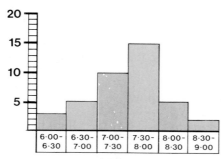

**Number of children (Total : 40)**

**Times people get up**

## 🖸 Listen

Karen works on the TV programme *Breakfast Time*. Listen to her talking about her routine, and complete the timetable.

| Time | Activity |
|---|---|
| ..... | She gets up and has a cup of coffee. |
| ..... | She takes a taxi to the studio. |
| 4.30 | ............................................. |
| ..... | She reads the programme notes. |
| 6.30 | The programme starts. |
| ..... | She watches a video of the programme. |
| 10.00 | She has lunch. |

## Write

Write a letter to a friend about your daily routine. Use the letter in Lesson 44 to help you.
*Paragraph 1*
Say what time you get up and what you have for breakfast.
*Paragraph 2*
Say what you usually do during the day, how many lessons you have and what you do in the breaks.
*Paragraph 3*
Say what activities you do after school and in the evenings. Say also what time you go to bed.

## 📻 Conversation

Complete the conversation with Andy. You are talking on the telephone.

ANDY: Hello. The weather's horrible here today. It's cold and wet. What's the weather like in your area today?

YOU: .........

ANDY: What time do you finish lessons in the afternoon?

YOU: .........

ANDY: What do you usually do after school?

YOU: .........

ANDY: Do you? I usually go to John's house and play table tennis. Anyway, what's the time now?

YOU: .........

ANDY: Is it? I must go. Bye!

YOU: .........

## Grammar Lessons 41-45

| How much | is | it?<br>an orange? | It's 45p. | | |
| | are | they?<br>the oranges? | They're | 40p<br>20p | a packet.<br>each. |

| I'm | hungry.<br>thirsty. | I'd like something to | eat.<br>drink. |

| What do you want? | Can I have<br>I'd like | some biscuits,<br>some lemonade, | please. |

| What time is it? | It's five o'clock. |

| What time is lunch? | It's at half past twelve. |

| What time<br>When | do<br>does he/she | you<br>they | get up?<br>go to bed? |

| I<br>We<br>They | get up<br>go to bed | at | eight o'clock.<br>9.30. |
| He/She gets up | | | |

| What | do<br>does he/she | you<br>they | do in the | morning?<br>afternoon?<br>evening? |

| I<br>We<br>They | usually<br>sometimes | go swimming.<br>go riding.<br>play tennis. |
| He/She | | plays tennis.<br>goes swimming. |

| What's the weather like? | It's | raining.<br>very cold. |

# What's 'goodbye' in Japanese?

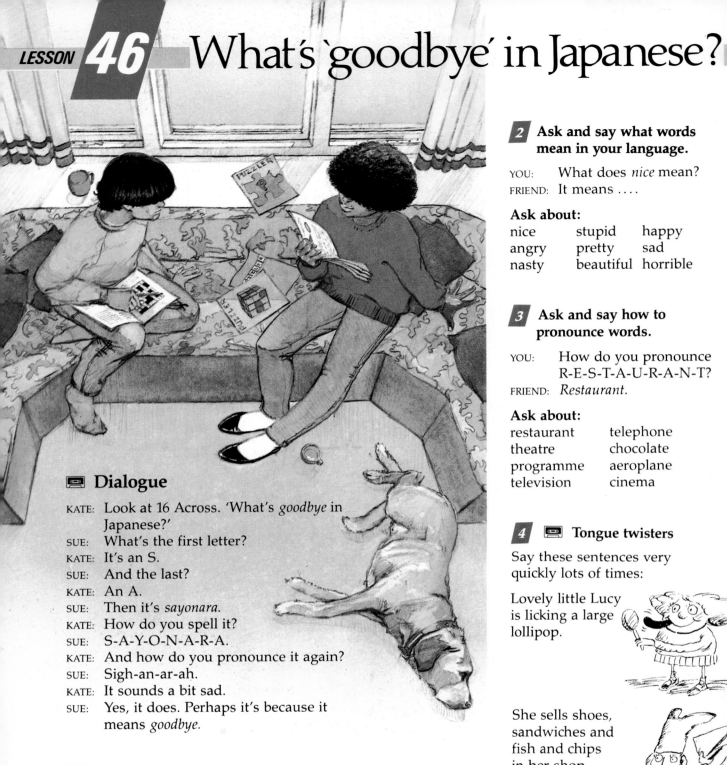

## 📼 Dialogue

KATE: Look at 16 Across. 'What's *goodbye* in Japanese?'
SUE: What's the first letter?
KATE: It's an S.
SUE: And the last?
KATE: An A.
SUE: Then it's *sayonara*.
KATE: How do you spell it?
SUE: S-A-Y-O-N-A-R-A.
KATE: And how do you pronounce it again?
SUE: Sigh-an-ar-ah.
KATE: It sounds a bit sad.
SUE: Yes, it does. Perhaps it's because it means *goodbye*.

---

**1** Ask and answer about words and phrases from other languages.

YOU: What's *goodbye* in Japanese?
FRIEND: It's *sayonara*./I don't know.

**Ask about:**

1. *goodbye* in Japanese.
2. *good morning* in French.
3. *good evening* in Greek.
4. *how are you?* in German.
5. *yes* and *no* in Russian.
6. *goodbye* in Spanish.
7. *hotel* in French.

---

**2** Ask and say what words mean in your language.

YOU: What does *nice* mean?
FRIEND: It means . . . .

**Ask about:**

| | | |
|---|---|---|
| nice | stupid | happy |
| angry | pretty | sad |
| nasty | beautiful | horrible |

---

**3** Ask and say how to pronounce words.

YOU: How do you pronounce R-E-S-T-A-U-R-A-N-T?
FRIEND: *Restaurant.*

**Ask about:**

| | |
|---|---|
| restaurant | telephone |
| theatre | chocolate |
| programme | aeroplane |
| television | cinema |

---

**4** 📼 Tongue twisters

Say these sentences very quickly lots of times:

Lovely little Lucy is licking a large lollipop.

She sells shoes, sandwiches and fish and chips in her shop in Sheffield.

---

**5** Are there any English words in your language? How many can you write down in a minute?

# When's your birthday?

## 🔊 Dialogue

KATE: When's your birthday?

SUE: It's in March. When's yours?

KATE: Mine's in the summer. It's on 22nd July.

SUE: What's the date today?

KATE: It's 11th May.

SUE: Oh, it's Miss Harris's birthday next Thursday. Let's collect some money and get her a present.

KATE: And a card!

SUE: OK. Let's tell the others ...

MRS TODD: Susan! Kate! This is a PE class, not a conversation class!

### 1 Answer the questions.

1. In which month is Sue's birthday?
2. In which season is Kate's birthday?
3. In which month is Kate's birthday?
4. On which day of the week is Miss Harris's birthday?

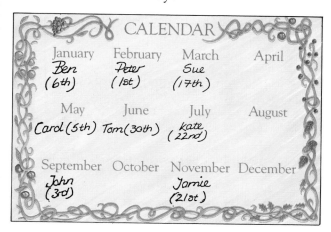

CALENDAR

| January | February | March | April |
|---------|----------|-------|-------|
| Ben (6th) | Peter (1st) | Sue (17th) | |
| May | June | July | August |
| Carol (5th) | Tom (30th) | Kate (22nd) | |
| September | October | November | December |
| John (3rd) | | Jamie (21st) | |

### 2 Use the calendar. Ask and say in which months people's birthdays are.

YOU: When's Kate's birthday?

FRIEND: It's in July. When's John's?

YOU: In September.

### 3 Practise saying the ordinal numbers.

| 1st first | 2nd second | 3rd third | 4th fourth | 5th fifth | 6th sixth |
|---|---|---|---|---|---|
| 7th seventh | 8th eighth | 9th ninth | 10th tenth | 11th eleventh | 12th twelfth |
| 13th thirteenth | 14th fourteenth | 15th fifteenth | 16th sixteenth | 17th seventeenth | 18th eighteenth |
| 19th nineteenth | 20th twentieth | 21st twenty-first | 29th twenty-ninth | 30th thirtieth | 31st thirty-first |

*Look!*

**in** March      **on** 14th March

We write *14th March*,

but we say '**the** fourteenth **of** March'.

### 4 Look at the calendar again and ask and answer about the dates of people's birthdays.

YOU: When's Ben's birthday?

FRIEND: It's on 6th January.

### 5 In groups, ask the dates of people's birthdays and make a birthday calendar for the class.

YOU: When's your birthday?

FRIEND: It's on 4th September.

### The seasons in Britain

| Spring | Summer | Autumn | Winter |
|--------|--------|--------|--------|
| March | June | September | December |
| April | July | October | January |
| May | August | November | February |

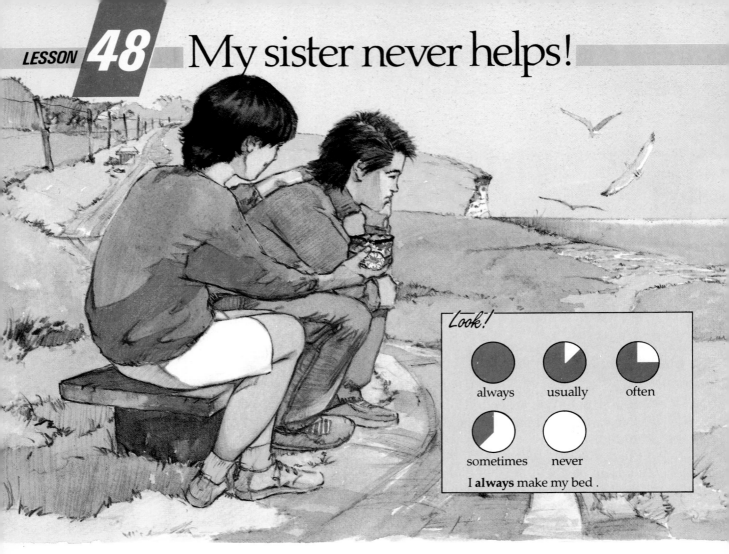

# LESSON 48 My sister never helps!

**Look!**

always    usually    often

sometimes    never

I **always** make my bed.

## 📼 Dialogue

KATE: What's the matter? Why are you sad?

JOHN: I'm not sad! I'm angry! I haven't got my pocket money this week.

KATE: Why not?

JOHN: My mum says I'm lazy and I don't help in the house.

KATE: Do you want some crisps?

JOHN: Thanks. It's not true. I help my mum quite a lot. My sister never helps! But I do.

KATE: I don't believe you!

JOHN: Well, I usually make my bed.

### 1  Correct the statements.

1. John is happy.
   No. He's angry.

1. John is happy.
2. John has got his pocket money this week.
3. John's sister helps in the house.
4. John always makes his bed.

### 2  Copy and complete the questionnaire on the right for yourself and for your partner.

YOU: Do you ever make your bed?

FRIEND: Yes, always.

### 3  Tell the class about one or two things you do in the house and how you spend your pocket money.

JOHN: I usually make my bed and I sometimes tidy my room. I never buy clothes with my pocket money.

### 4  Say how much John helps in the house.

YOU: He usually makes his bed.

FRIEND: And he sometimes tidies his room.

### Now say what he does with his pocket money.

YOU: He never buys clothes.

FRIEND: And he never buys records or cassettes.

75 (seventy-five)

# Do you help in the house? (Tell the truth!)

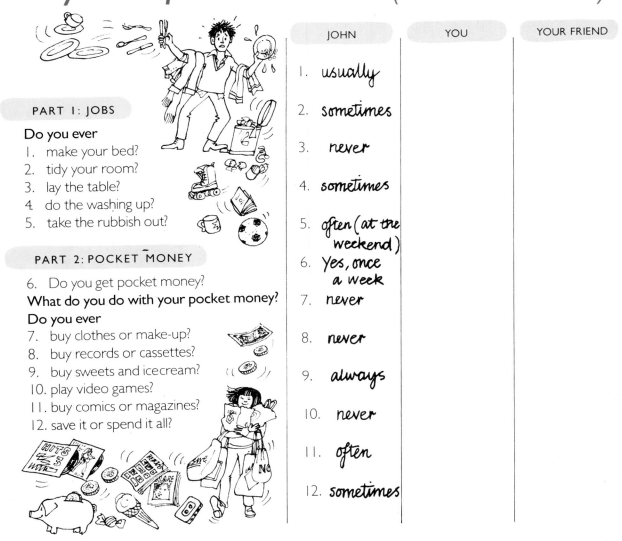

### PART 1: JOBS

**Do you ever**

1. make your bed?
2. tidy your room?
3. lay the table?
4. do the washing up?
5. take the rubbish out?

### PART 2: POCKET MONEY

6. Do you get pocket money?

**What do you do with your pocket money?**

**Do you ever**

7. buy clothes or make-up?
8. buy records or cassettes?
9. buy sweets and icecream?
10. play video games?
11. buy comics or magazines?
12. save it or spend it all?

| JOHN | YOU | YOUR FRIEND |
|---|---|---|
| 1. usually | | |
| 2. sometimes | | |
| 3. never | | |
| 4. sometimes | | |
| 5. often (at the weekend) | | |
| 6. Yes, once a week | | |
| 7. never | | |
| 8. never | | |
| 9. always | | |
| 10. never | | |
| 11. often | | |
| 12. sometimes | | |

**5** **Look at what John says.**

'I help my mother quite a lot in the house.
I usually make my bed and I sometimes tidy
my room – usually on Saturday morning.
I sometimes do the washing up and often take
the rubbish out at the weekend.

I usually get pocket money once a week. I
always buy a few sweets and icecream. I never
spend it on clothes or records or cassettes but
I often buy comics. I sometimes save a little
because I want to buy a canoe.'

**Now write two paragraphs about John.**

John helps his mother quite a lot in the house.

**6** **Write one paragraph about the jobs you
do and don't do in the house, and another
paragraph about how you spend your
pocket money.**

# Does she like chocolates?

### 📼 Dialogue

SUE: What shall we buy Miss Harris for her birthday? Does she like chocolates?

KATE: Yes, she does. But that's not a very interesting present.

SUE: She likes house plants. Let's get her a rubber plant.

KATE: How much are they?

SUE: Look, they're £6. They're too expensive.

KATE: Let's get her some writing paper and envelopes. She likes writing letters.

SUE: OK. That's £2.20. We've got an extra 50p.

KATE: Hey, Sue! Let's get her a vampire bat as well!

### 1 True or False?

Miss Harris:
1. doesn't like chocolates.
2. likes house plants.
3. doesn't like writing letters.

## 2 Find out what your partner likes and doesn't like.

YOU: Do you like yogurt?
FRIEND: Yes, I do./No, I don't.

### FOOD AND DRINK

yogurt    milk chocolate    fish soup

### INTERESTS

computer games    ballet    classical music

### ANIMALS AND REPTILES

snakes    rats    crocodiles

## 3 Ask someone else in the class about their partner.

YOU: Does Peter like milk chocolate?
FRIEND: No, he doesn't.

## 4 Look at what Sue writes about Miss Harris.

*Miss Harris likes chocolates, houseplants and opera. She doesn't like pop music or dogs.*

**Write similar sentences about your friend's likes and dislikes.**

## 5 Choose a birthday present for Kate, Andy, Mr Green and Miss Harris.

YOU: It's Kate's/Andy's birthday next week. What shall we get her/him?
FRIEND: Let's get her/him a present.
YOU: What sort of present?
FRIEND: Let's get her/him a jigsaw.
YOU: No, let's get her/him a game.

a scarf    a jigsaw    a mug    a game

tights

a box of    a house    a brush and
chocolates    plant    comb set

## 6 The hidden present

Sue and Kate buy another small present for Miss Harris. Write down the first letter of each item to find out what the present is.

1.    2.    3.    4.

5.    6.    7.    8.

## 🔊 Birthday song

Happy birthday to you!
Happy birthday to you!
Happy birthday Miss Harris!
Happy birthday to you!

**Read**

Discoveries meets... **ANNE McCRODDEN**

T R A I N E E   E N G I N E E R

When Anne gets up in the morning she puts on an overall and big boots and she carries a helmet—because she's training to be an engineer.

'I am a trainee on a three-year course. I am now in my third year. I am enjoying the course very much. I like making things and I like technical subjects. I think I'm lucky to have something to do. A lot of people think it's strange for a girl to be an engineer. I don't. A lot of my friends laugh at me, but they either have very boring jobs or they are unemployed.

After work at nights I like going to discos and night clubs. I always tell the boys I'm an engineer. They are sometimes rude and say, "Where are your overalls, Jack?" and walk away, but I don't mind. I usually go to the disco with the boys from my course. *They* laugh because I am wearing evening clothes.

At the end of my course I want a job with London Transport because I like trains. Do you know what I want for my birthday? A new helmet!'

**Choose the correct answer.**

1. When Anne gets dressed she:
   a) puts on a dress.
   b) puts on an overall.

2. Anne:
   a) likes her course very much.
   b) thinks her course is strange.

3. People laugh at Anne because:
   a) she is funny.
   b) they think engineering is a strange job for a girl.

4. Some of Anne's other friends:
   a) have no job.
   b) are boring.

5. In discos, boys are:
   a) usually rude to Jack.
   c) sometimes rude to Anne.

**Write**

1. Write about the daily routine of an adult you know – a parent, a relative or a friend of the family. Or imagine the life of a famous person.

*Paragraph 1*
Say what time the person gets up and what he or she usually has for breakfast.
*Paragraph 2*
Write three or four sentences about what the person does during the day.
*Paragraph 3*
Say one or two things about the person's routine in the evening and say what he or she has for supper.
**or**
2. Describe how you usually spend your birthday.

## ▣ Conversation

Complete the conversation with John.

JOHN: When's your birthday?
YOU: . . . . . . . . . .
JOHN: Mine's next month. I want a tent for my birthday. What do you want for yours?
YOU: . . . . . . . . . .
JOHN: Do you? How much pocket money do you get a week?
YOU: . . . . . . . . . .
JOHN: What do you do with it?
YOU: . . . . . . . . . .
JOHN: I buy comics and sweets! I get more money if I help my mother in the house. Do you help in the home?
YOU: . . . . . . . . . .

JOHN: Does your mother tidy your room?
YOU: . . . . . . . . . .
JOHN: Oh, there's my dad calling me. Bye!
YOU: . . . . . . . . . .

## ▣ Listen

Listen to Jenny and Mickey talking about jobs in the house. Look at the list below and tick the jobs which they do.

take the rubbish out            tidy her/his room
go shopping                     wash up
make the beds                   lay the table
take the dog for a walk         do some cooking

## Grammar Lessons 46-50

| What date is / When's | your birthday? | | It's | in | October. / the summer. |
| --- | --- | --- | --- | --- | --- |
| | | | | on | Monday. / October 10th. |

| What's | the | date | today? | | It's | Monday, July 3rd. / July 3rd. / 3rd July. |
| --- | --- | --- | --- | --- | --- | --- |

| Do you | ever / always / often | help in the home? | | I / She / He | always usually often sometimes never | make my / makes | her / his | bed. |
| --- | --- | --- | --- | --- | --- | --- | --- | --- |

| Does he/she like cats? | Yes, / No, | he/she | does. / doesn't. | | He/She | likes / doesn't like | cats. |
| --- | --- | --- | --- | --- | --- | --- | --- |

| What shall we | buy / get | Miss Harris/her? / Mr Green/him? | | Let's | buy / get | Miss Harris/her / Mr Green/him | a present. |
| --- | --- | --- | --- | --- | --- | --- | --- |

| What's / What does | au revoir | in English? / mean in English? | | It's / It means | goodbye. |
| --- | --- | --- | --- | --- | --- |

# Oral exercises

## LESSONS 1-5

### 1. Greet and say goodbye to people
Say hello to Kate.
*Hello, Kate.*
Say goodbye to John.
*Goodbye, John.*

| | |
|---|---|
| 1. Kate | 4. Miss Harris |
| 2. John | 5. Mr Green |
| 3. Cleo | 6. Mrs Morgan |

### 2. Greet someone and introduce yourself (Open exercise)
Greet Kate.
*Hello, Kate. (I'm Mary.)*

| | |
|---|---|
| 1. Kate | 4. Miss Harris |
| 2. Mr Green | 5. John |
| 3. Mrs Morgan | 6. Andy |

### 3. Introduce yourself and ask someone's name
You are John.
*I'm John. What's your name?*

| | |
|---|---|
| 1. John | 4. Mary |
| 2. Max | 5. Peter |
| 3. Tina | |

### 4. Introduce your family to Tina
Introduce your mother.
*Hi, Tina. This is my mother.*

| | |
|---|---|
| 1. mother | 3. little brother |
| 2. father | 4. sister |

### 5. Introduce yourself
Hello.
*Hello. I'm Tina's brother.*

| | |
|---|---|
| 1. Tina/brother | 4. Anna/teacher |
| 2. John/mother | 5. Pat/father |
| 3. Pat/teacher | 6. Anna/friend |

### 6. Give people's names
Who's that?
*That's Prince Charles.*
What's his name?
*That's Stevie Wonder.*

| | |
|---|---|
| 1. Prince Charles | 4. Princess Diana |
| 2. Stevie Wonder | 5. Michael Jackson |
| 3. Margaret Thatcher | 6. Tarzan |

## LESSONS 6-10

### 1. Ask for personal information
*What's your telephone number?*
It's 149623.
*What's Mary's favourite number?*
It's 7.

1. Your telephone number?
2. Mary's favourite number?
3. Andy's address?
4. Kate's favourite number?
5. Jack's address?
6. Tina's telephone number?

### 2. Ask people's age
*Is she six?*
No, but she's nearly six.

| | |
|---|---|
| 1. she six? | 5. your sister nine? |
| 2. he eleven? | 6. your father forty? |
| 3. you twelve? | |
| 4. your brother sixteen? | |

### 3. Ask how old people are
*How old is Tina?*
She's twelve.

| | | |
|---|---|---|
| 1. Tina? | 3. she? | 5. Mark? |
| 2. he? | 4. Miss Harris? | |

### 4. Answer questions about objects
Is number one a computer?
*Yes, it is.*
Is number two a pen?
*No, it isn't. It's a pencil.*

| | |
|---|---|
| 1. computer/yes | 4. cat/yes |
| 2. pen/no/pencil | 5. ruler/no/rubber |
| 3. comic/no/notebook | 6. calculator/yes |

### 5. Identify objects
What's that?
*It's my ruler.*

| | |
|---|---|
| 1. my ruler | 5. Sue's cassette recorder |
| 2. Andy's pen | |
| 3. Kate's notebook | 6. Mr Green's pen |
| 4. my calculator | |

### 6. Give information about animals
What's that animal?
*It's an African elephant.*

| | |
|---|---|
| 1. African elephant | 4. Indian tiger |
| 2. Chinese panda | 5. English sheep dog |
| 3. American bald eagle | |

## LESSONS 11-15

### 1. Say where people are from
Where's Eddie Murphy from?
*He's from the USA.*

1. Eddie Murphy/USA
2. Isabelle Huppert/France
3. Sophia Loren/Italy
4. Severiano Ballesteros/Spain
5. Daley Thompson/Britain

### 2. Correct information about nationalities
Is Harrison Ford British?
*No, he isn't. He's American.*

1. Harrison Ford/American
2. Sophia Loren/Italian
3. Daley Thompson/British
4. Isabelle Huppert/French
5. Severiano Ballesteros/Spanish

### 3. Say where places are
Where's Peking?
*It's in China.*

1. Peking/China
2. Rio de Janeiro/Brazil
3. Buenos Aires/Argentina
4. Tokyo/Japan
5. Munich/West Germany

### 4. Ask about nationalities
*Are you Spanish?*
No, we aren't. We're Greek.

| | |
|---|---|
| 1. Spanish? | 4. Brazilian? |
| 2. American? | 5. Argentinian? |
| 3. Italian? | |

### 5. Make suitable responses (Open exercise)
Sorry.
*(That's OK.)*

| | |
|---|---|
| 1. Sorry. | 4. Thanks very much. |
| 2. Here you are. | 5. Do you want a chocolate? |
| 3. Goodbye. | |

### 6. Offer people things
Offer your friend a chocolate.
*Do you want a chocolate?*

| | |
|---|---|
| 1. a chocolate? | 4. an icecream? |
| 2. some crisps? | 5. some chewing gum? |
| 3. some sweets? | |

### 7. Say what the colours are
What colour is Pat's hair?
*It's blonde.*
What colour are her eyes?
*They're blue.*

1. Pat's hair/blonde
2. her eyes/blue
3. Peter's hair/black
4. his eyes/brown
5. Anna's hair/blonde
6. her eyes/green

## LESSONS 16-20

### 1. Ask whose belongings you have
sweater
*Whose sweater is this?*
trainers
*Whose trainers are these?*

| | |
|---|---|
| 1. sweater? | 4. socks? |
| 2. trainers? | 5. shoes? |
| 3. jacket? | 6. anorak? |

### 2. Correct information about belongings
Is this Jane's?
*No, it isn't hers. It's mine.*
Are these John's?
*No, they aren't his. They're mine.*

| | |
|---|---|
| 1. this Jane's | 4. these Robert's |
| 2. these John's | 5. this Kate's |
| 3. this Linda's | 6. this Andy's |

### 3. Agree with people's tastes
I like Harrison Ford.
*Yes, I like him, too.*
I like Nastassia Kinski.
*Yes, I like her, too.*

| | |
|---|---|
| 1. Harrison Ford | 4. Wham! |
| 2. Nastassia Kinski | 5. Sophia Loren |
| 3. The Jackson Five | 6. Stevie Wonder |

### 4. Say who you like and don't like
I like Michael Jackson. I think he's terrific.
*Oh, I don't like him. I think he's horrible.*
I don't like Madonna. I think she's boring.
*Oh, I like her. I think she's fantastic.*

1. I like Michael Jackson. I think he's terrific.
2. I don't like Madonna. I think she's boring.
3. I like Julian Lennon. I think he's terrific.
4. I don't like Billy Idol. I think he's boring.
5. I like Tina Turner. I think she's terrific.
6. I don't like Adam Ant. I think he's boring.

### 5. Say what you've got and what you haven't got
stamps and badges
*I've got some stamps but I haven't got any badges.*

1. stamps/badges
2. records/posters
3. French stamps/Italian stamps
4. foreign postcards/foreign coins
5. sweets/crisps

### 6. Make an offer or a refusal
Have you got any postcards?
*Yes, I have. Do you want one?*
Have you got any stamps?
*No, I haven't. Sorry.*

| | |
|---|---|
| 1. postcards/yes | 4. crisps/yes |
| 2. stamps/no | 5. chocolates/no |
| 3. pencils/yes | 6. sweets/no |

### 7. Ask how many
She's got lots of stamps.
*Oh? How many has she got?*
I've got lots of records.
*Oh? How many have you got?*

| | |
|---|---|
| 1. She/stamps | 4. Anna/posters |
| 2. I/records | 5. Mary/badges |
| 3. Jack/videos | 6. I/pets |

## LESSONS 21-25

### Ask about numbers
*How many people are there in your family?*
There are six.

1. people/in your family?
2. students/in your class?
3. girls/in your class?
4. boys/in your class?
5. teachers/in your school?
6. posters/in your bedroom?

### 2. Ask about rooms in a house
*Is there a kitchen in your house?*
Yes, there is.

| | |
|---|---|
| 1. kitchen? | 4. bathroom? |
| 2. dining room? | 5. play room? |
| 3. attic? | 6. sitting room? |

### 3. Talk about the furniture in a room
Is there a bed?
*Oh yes, there's a very nice bed.*
Are there any curtains?
*Oh yes, there are some very nice curtains.*

| | |
|---|---|
| 1. bed | 4. posters |
| 2. curtains | 5. chairs |
| 3. table | 6. cupboard |

### 4. Comment on places
Are there any castles in France?
*Yes, there are some beautiful castles in France.*

1. castles in France
2. churches in London
3. gardens in Paris
4. cliffs in Dover
5. Roman remains in Italy
6. places to see in your country

### 5. Talk about places
Tell me about Canterbury.
*It's a city in the south-east of England.*
Tell me about Los Angeles.
*It's a city on the west coast of the USA.*

1. Canterbury/south-east/England
2. Los Angeles/west coast/USA
3. Aberdeen/east coast/Scotland
4. Cambridge/east/England
5. Bordeaux/south-west coast/France
6. Cardiff/south coast/Wales

### 6. Answer personal questions
 (Open exercise)
What's your name, please?
*(John Smith.)*

1. What's your name, please?
2. What's your address?
3. And your telephone number?
4. Where are you from?
5. How old are you?
6. What are your parents' names?
7. What colour is your hair?
8. What colour are your eyes?

## LESSONS 26-30

### 1. Spell words in English
 (Open exercise)
Spell the name of your country.
*(E-N-G-L-A-N-D)*

1. the name of your country
2. the name of your capital city
3. your best friend's surname
4. your first name
5. the name of your favourite pop singer or group

### 2. Ask what people are doing
I'm listening to records.
*Are you? What are you listening to?*
I'm reading.
*Are you? What are you reading?*

| | |
|---|---|
| 1. listening to records | 4. writing |
| 2. reading | 5. eating |
| 3. watching TV | 6. drinking |

**3. Give short answers**
Are they doing their homework?
*Yes, they are.*
Is she playing basketball?
*No, she isn't.*

1. they/do homework/yes
2. she/play basketball/no
3. he/play with dog/yes
4. they/watch TV/no
5. she/make model trains/no
6. he/ride bike/yes

**4. Say what people are doing**
What are they doing?
*They're singing.*
What's he doing?
*He's running.*

1. They          4. He
2. He            5. They
3. She           6. They

## LESSONS 31-35

**1. Ask what people like**
Ask Andy about cheeseburgers.
*Do you like cheeseburgers, Andy?*

1. cheeseburgers, Andy?
2. mustard, Kate?
3. chocolate milkshakes, Lucy?
4. milk, Sue?
5. tomato ketchup, John?
6. fish, Tom?

**2. Say what you like** (Open exercise)
Do you like hamburgers with onions?
*(Yes, I do.)*
Do you like coffee?
*(No, I don't.)*

1. hamburgers       4. tea without sugar?
   with onions?     5. tomato ketchup?
2. coffee?          6. lots of pepper on
3. bananas?            your food?

**3. Ask people to identify the objects
   they like**
Oh, look, that tracksuit's nice.
*Which one do you mean?*
Oh, look, those trainers are good.
*Which ones do you mean?*

1. tracksuit/nice    4. anorak/nice
2. trainers/good     5. shoes/good
3. T-shirt/nice      6. school bag/nice

**4. Say what people like and don't like**
Tina
*Tina likes chips but she doesn't like fish.*

1. Tina/chips/fish
2. Jack/hamburgers/cheeseburgers
3. Max/milk/tea
4. Mrs Brown/sailing/swimming
5. Mr Brown/skiing/waterskiing
6. Anna/Tina/Jack

**5. Ask about your school timetable**
English
*When have we got English?*
Science on Friday
*Have we got Science on Friday?*

1. When/English?     4. Have/Games
2. Have/Science         on Thursday?
   on Friday?        5. When/Music?
3. Have/Biology      6. When/Maths?
   on Monday?

**6. Answer about your school timetable**
   (Open exercise)
Have you got English on Thursday?
*(Yes, we have.)*
Have you got Maths every day?
*(No, we haven't.)*

1. Have you got English on Thursday?
2. Have you got Maths every day?
3. Have you got Music on Tuesday?
4. Have you got Science on Friday?
5. Have you got History on
   Wednesday?
6. Have you got English today?

**7. Answer about your interests**
   (Open exercise)
Do you like canoeing?
*(No, I don't.)*
Do you like watching TV?
*(Yes, I do.)*

1. canoeing          4. singing
2. watching TV       5. learning English
3. writing letters   6. doing Maths

**8. Talk about your interests and
   activities** (Open exercise)
What subjects to you like learning
at school?
*(I like learning Geography and English.)*

1. What subjects do you like learning
   at school?
2. What do you like doing at the
   weekend?
3. What do you like doing after school?

**4. Do you like doing homework?**
5. What programmes do you like
   watching on TV?
6. When you are with your friends,
   what do you like doing?

## LESSONS 36-40

**1. Give a different opinion**
I think it's a beautiful picture.
*Oh, I don't think it's beautiful. I think
it's ugly.*

1. picture/beautiful/ugly
2. man/clever/stupid
3. woman/nice/horrid
4. toy/expensive/cheap
5. car/fast/slow
6. house/small/big

**2. Say what the matter is with things**
What's the matter with your tea?
*It's too hot.*

1. tea/too hot       4. chair/too hard
2. soup/too cold     5. hotel room/too
3. homework/too         noisy
   difficult

**3. Describe how you are doing things**
Come on! Do it quickly.
*I am doing it quickly!*

1. Come on! Do it quickly.
2. Ssh! Sing softly.
3. Come on! Speak loudly.
4. Wait a moment! Say it clearly.
5. Please drive slowly!
6. Ssh! Play quietly!

**4. Follow instructions**
Say 'Hello' loudly.
*HELLO!*

1. Say 'Hello' loudly.
2. Say 'Thank you very much' quietly.
3. Say 'No, I don't' slowly.
4. Say 'I hate you' nastily.
5. Say 'Be quiet and go away, Lucy'
   very quickly.
6. Say the name of your best friend
   quietly.

**5. Ask questions about size**

nice garden
*It's a nice garden. How wide is it?*
big swimming pool
*It's a big swimming pool. How deep is it?*

1. nice garden/wide?
2. big swimming pool/deep?
3. big building/tall?
4. big bridge/long?
5. enormous mountain/high?
6. wide river/deep?

## LESSONS 41-45

**1. Ask for things to eat and drink**

Ask for two Cokes.
*Can I have two Cokes, please?*

1. two Cokes
2. a glass of milk
3. a packet of crisps
4. two bottles of lemonade
5. a chocolate egg
6. a glass of orange juice

**2. Say the price of things**

How much is the torch?
*It's two pounds eighty.*
How much are the postcards?
*They're twenty p.*

1. the torch/£2.80
2. the postcards/20p
3. the writing paper/£1.75
4. a packet of sweets/54p
5. the stickers/10p

**3. Give times of arrival**

What time does the train arrive?
*It arrives at five o'clock.*

1. train/five o'clock
2. plane/half past four
3. boat/quarter past four
4. hovercraft/half past three
5. bus/nine o'clock
6. train/quarter past seven

**4. Say what time it is**

What's the time, please?
*It's five to ten.*

1.    2.    3.

4.    5.    6.

**5. Ask about routines**

Glenda is a famous film star. Ask her about her daily timetable.
Ask her what time she gets up.
*What time do you get up Miss Glenning?*
Get up? How horrible. I get up at half past eleven.

1. What time/get up?
2. What time/have breakfast?
3. Where/have lunch?
4. What/have for lunch?
5. What time/go to the studios?
6. When/go to bed?

**6. Answer questions about your daily routine** (Open exercise)

What time do you usually get up in the morning?
*I usually get up at half past seven.*

1. What time do you usually get up in the morning?
2. What about on Saturday and Sunday?
3. Do you get dressed before breakfast or after breakfast?
4. What do you usually have for breakfast?
5. Where do you have lunch?
6. What do you usually do in the evenings?
7. What time do you go to bed?
8. Do you read in bed?

**7. Say what the weather is like**

What's the weather like in Rome today?
*It's sunny.*

1. Rome/sunny
2. London/sunny
3. Berlin/cloudy
4. Stockholm/snowing
5. New York/raining
6. Malta/raining

## LESSONS 46-50

**1. Answer about birthdays**

When's Ben's birthday?
*It's some time in the winter.*
Do you know when?
*I think it's in January.*

1. Ben/winter/January
2. Carol/spring/May
3. Kate/summer/July
4. John/autumn/September
5. Sue/spring/March
6. Tom/summer/June

**2. Give exact dates of birthdays**

When's John's birthday?
*It's on the third of September.*

1. John/3rd September
2. Jamie/21st November
3. Mary/12th January
4. Kevin/31st March
5. Sheila/24th October
6. Mr Morgan/11th December

**3. Say what the date is** (Open exercise)

What's the date today?
*(It's the fifth of April.)*

1. What's the date today?
2. What's the date tomorrow?
3. What date's your birthday?
4. What date's your best friend's birthday?
5. What date's your next English class?
6. What date's the start of the school holidays?

**4. Ask about the spelling and meaning of words.**

*How do you spell 'beautiful'?*
B-E-A-U-T-I-F-U-L
*What does 'intelligent' mean?*
That you are clever.

1. How/spell 'beautiful'?
2. What/'intelligent' mean?
3. What/'helmet' mean?
4. How/spell 'technical'?
5. What/'strange' mean?
6. How/spell 'frightened'?

**5. Ask about the things Miss Harris likes**

*Does Miss Harris like plants?*
Yes, she does.
*Does she like video games?*
No, she doesn't.

1. plants?
2. video games?
3. snakes?
4. peanut butter?
5. classical music?
6. chocolate?

# Words and expressions

## LESSON 1

my
your
and
Hello.
name
What?
be (is)
*cardinal numbers*
1-10

## LESSON 2

Good afternoon.
Good evening.
Good morning.
Goodbye.

friend
picture
teacher

under

I

be (am)

*titles*
Miss
Mr
Mrs

*family members*
brother
father
mother
sister

## LESSON 3

OK.
little

a

Hi.
I'm OK, thanks.

no
yes

dad
school
twins
witch

from
he
she
this
we
you
How?

go away
know (a person)
be (are)

## LESSON 4

called
her
his

our

but

I must go.
Bye.

cat
dog
mum
teatime

that

Who?

## LESSON 5

me

have

## LESSON 6

young

nearly
only
too

Come on.
Let's…

years old

How old?

go
want

*cardinal numbers*
11-20

## LESSON 7

favourite
new
old

the

Say it again slowly.

address book
number
telephone

it

look at

*cardinal numbers*
20-101

## LESSON 8

book
calculator
cassette recorder
chair
comic
computer
desk
notebook
pen
pencil
rubber
ruler
stool
table

## LESSON 9

big
good
its
wrong

Thank you.

animal
ears
knees
page
picture

next

Where?

know

*animals*
eagle
elephant
lion
panda
sheep dog
tiger

*countries and
    nationalities*
Africa (African)
China (Chinese)
England (English)
India (Indian)
North America
    (American)

## LESSON 10

wild

today
city
pet

has

## LESSON 11

man (*pl* men)
nationality
woman (*pl* women)

in

*countries and
    nationalities*
Britain (British)
France (French)
Italy (Italian)
Spain (Spanish)
The USA (American)

## LESSON 12

silly

It doesn't matter.
Look out!
Sorry.
That's OK.

boy
children (*sing* child)
girl
parent

*countries and
    nationalities*
Argentina
    (Argentinian)
Brazil (Brazilian)
Germany (German)
Greece (Greek)
Japan (Japanese)
Turkey (Turkish)

## LESSON 13

some

Here you are.
Thanks (very much).
No, thank you.
Yes, please.

for

hate
love

*food*
chewing gum
chocolates
crisps
icecream
liquorice
sweet

## LESSON 14

bright
dark
light

apple
banana
cloud
colour
eyes
grass
hair
orange
sea
sky
sun
tomato
tree

What colour?

*colours*
black
blonde
blue
brown
grey

orange
pink
purple
red
white
yellow

## LESSON 15

good-looking

doctor
schoolgirl

## LESSON 16

here
perhaps

Don't be cheeky!

hers
his
mine
these
this
yours

Whose?

Why?

*clothes*
anorak
blouse
boots
coat
dress
jacket
jeans
shirt
shoes
skirt
socks
sweater
trainers
trousers
T-shirt

## LESSON 17

bad
boring
fantastic
funny
great
horrible
purple
their

band
pop music
pop star
record

her
him
them

like
think

## LESSON 18

gold

or

Great!
Let's see it.

bike
camera
football
radio
sleeping bag
snake
stamp album
tennis racket
tent
watch
wheel

over there

one

have got

## LESSON 19

any
foreign
model

badge
coin
collection
cousin
postcard
poster
sticker
train

How many?

## LESSON 20

quiet
shy

album
member
sequin
sheep

dance
swap

*family members*
aunt
uncle

## LESSON 21

altogether

Guess what.

people
thousand

over
under
with

a lot

## LESSON 22

best
small

opposite

theirs

*house*
attic
bathroom
bedroom
dining room
downstairs
floor
ground floor
kitchen
play room
roof
sitting room
toilet
upstairs

## LESSON 23

afraid of
alone
dark
enormous
full of
private
spooky

because

bird's nest
box
dolls
flag
game
ghost
lock
notice
photo
spider
team
thing
toy
typewriter

next to
on

*house*
bed
box
carpet
chimney
corner
cupboard
curtains
door
wall
window

## LESSON 24

busy
chalk
historical
important
interesting
large

boats
car ferries
castle
centre
cliffs
coast
flower
garden

hovercraft
letter
lighthouse
penfriend
place
port
remains
town

between
for
near

live

*compass points*
east
north
north-east
north-west
south
south-east
west

## LESSON 25

quite
somewhere

flat
stairs
waiter

into
on the top of
over

show

## LESSON 26

anything else

alphabet
bicycle lamp
brush
capital
comb
headmaster
headmistress
pair of scissors
penknife
president
purse
surname
torch
wallet

spell
want

## LESSON 27

sport
terrific

fast
very well

breath
champion
competition
guitar
hand
head
horse
omelette
piano
rope
water

can
climb
dive
draw
hold
knit
make
move
play
ride
run
send
sing
speak
stand
swim
use
walk

## LESSON 28

Be quiet!
Mind your own
   business.

girlfriend
hot chocolate
toffee
TV (television)

do
listen to
play with
talk to

## LESSON 29

first
last
second
third
unlucky

I don't understand.

ankle
basketball
football
leg
metre
race
scarf
tennis
volleyball

round

sit down
stand up
tie
wear

## LESSON 30

diamond
giant

Scotland
Wales
beach
belt
birdwatching
coast guard
gang
gun
island
lighthouse
packet
police
puffin
signal
smuggler
tortoise
village
wetsuit

drop
fall
fish
fly
help
row

## LESSON 31

just

either

without

weigh

*food*
Coca-Cola
apple pie
banana

cheeseburger
chicken
chips
coffee
cup
fish
hamburger
ketchup
menu
milk
milkshake
mustard
onions
orange juice
pepper
Pepsi Cola
salt
strawberry
tea
tomato soup

## LESSON 32

nice
silver
these (*adj*)
those (*adj*)

really

sports bag

these (*pron*)
those (*pron*)

Which?

*clothes*
roller skates
shorts
track suit

## LESSON 33

every

afternoon
break
lunch
morning
subject
timetable
weekend

When?

*days of the week*

*school subjects*
Art
Biology
Computer Studies
Current Affairs
Drama

French
Games
Geography
History
Home Economics
Library
Maths
Music
PE
RE
Science

## LESSON 34

perfect

neither

activity
adventure
badminton
free time
gymnastics
hole
museum
plate

by

act
canoe
join
paint
put
sail
scuba dive
ski
water ski
windsurf

## LESSON 35

elder
married
super

airport
ambulance driver
customs officer
flavour
group
hamburger bar
hospital
physics

## LESSON 36

beautiful
cheap
clean
clever
dirty

expensive
fat
friendly
golden
hard
long
pretty
short
slow
soft
thin
ugly
unfriendly
young

a bit
sometimes

fur
guard
neck
nose
shell
spots
stripes
tail

What sort?

*animals*
anteater
giant crab
giraffe
kitten
koala bear
Labrador
leopard
spider monkey
tortoise
zebra

## LESSON 37

cold
dangerous
difficult
easy
frightened
heavy
high
hot
light
low
nasty
noisy
safe
next door
quite

branch
ladder

someone
bring
chase
get down
hang on
let go
reach
slip

### LESSON 38

happy
loud

at first
at last
clearly
loudly
nastily
nicely
quickly
quietly
slowly

so

Wait a moment.

programme
seat
speech

get dressed
go on
hear
need
shut
smile
turn off
welcome

### LESSON 39

at least
deep
exactly
far
more than
shallow
special
tall
wide

Gosh!

bridge
building
centimetre
depth
distance
earth
end
fact

finger
foot/feet
half
height
inch
kilometre
length
mile
millimetre
million
moon
mountain
ocean
pyramid
quarter
river
swimming pool
tower
width

How (far) (deep)?

### LESSON 40

either…or
fourth
old-fashioned
popular
real life
rich
well known

always

character
soap opera

nothing

### LESSON 41

activity
each
hungry
thirsty
already

It's time to go.
Hurry up!

holiday
money
pence
pound
price
station
week

something

both
how much

drink

eat

*food and drink*
apple
biscuit
lemonade
nut
orange
peach

### LESSON 42

bored
lucky
tired

half past
quarter past
quarter to
tonight
usually

bedtime
journey
o'clock
supper

What time?

arrive

### LESSON 43

cloudy
dull
freezing
sunny
warm
wet

anyway

on average

hour
lightning
rain
snow
weather

behind
up there

go out
rain
shine
snow

### LESSON 44

homesick

autograph book
disco
mini-motorbike

monitor
shower
sort

*food*
bacon
cereal
egg
marmalade
porridge
sausage
toast

### LESSON 45

fine

cricket
crop
farm
meal
season
spring
summer

die

### LESSON 46

sad

across

aeroplane
cinema
lollipop
restaurant
theatre

lick
mean
pronounce
sell
sound

### LESSON 47

bossy

autumn
birthday
calendar
card
date
present
winter

others

collect
get

*months of the year*
January - December
*ordinal numbers*
1st - 31st

### LESSON 48

angry
crazy
lazy
true

a little

always
ever
never
often
sometimes

magazine
make-up
pocket money
rubbish
truth

believe
do the washing up
save
spend
tidy

### LESSON 49

extra

ballet
classical music
crocodile
dictionary
envelope
house plant
jigsaw
mug
opera
rat
scarf
soap
tights
writing paper

### LESSON 50

rude
strange
technical
unemployed

I don't mind.

course
engineer
helmet
night club
overall
trainee

laugh at
take for a walk

# Common irregular verbs

These verbs are in their infinitive/past tense/past participle forms.

## VERBS WITH NO CHANGE

| | | |
|---|---|---|
| cost | cost | cost |
| cut | cut | cut |
| hit | hit | hit |
| let | let | let |
| put | put | put |
| shut | shut | shut |

## VERBS WITH ONE CHANGE

| | | |
|---|---|---|
| bring | brought | brought |
| build | built | built |
| buy | bought | bought |
| catch | caught | caught |
| feel | felt | felt |
| find | found | found |
| get | got | got |
| hang | hung | hung |
| have | had | had |
| hear | heard | heard |
| hold | held | held |
| keep | kept | kept |
| learn | learnt | learnt |
| leave | left | left |
| lend | lent | lent |
| lose | lost | lost |
| make | made | made |
| mean | meant | meant |
| meet | met | met |
| pay | paid | paid |
| read | read | read |
| say | said | said |
| sell | sold | sold |
| send | sent | sent |
| shine | shone | shone |
| sit | sat | sat |
| sleep | slept | slept |
| spell | spelled/spelt | spelled/spelt |
| spend | spent | spent |
| stand | stood | stood |
| tell | told | told |
| think | thought | thought |
| understand | understood | understood |
| win | won | won |

## VERBS WITH TWO CHANGES

| | | |
|---|---|---|
| be | was | been |
| begin | began | begun |
| break | broke | broken |
| choose | chose | chosen |
| come | came | come |
| do | did | done |
| draw | drew | drawn |
| drink | drank | drunk |
| drive | drove | driven |
| eat | ate | eaten |
| fall | fell | fallen |
| fly | flew | flown |
| forget | forgot | forgotten |
| give | gave | given |
| go | went | gone |
| grow | grew | grown |
| know | knew | known |
| lie | lay | lain |
| ride | rode | ridden |
| ring | rang | rung |
| run | ran | run |
| see | saw | seen |
| show | showed | shown |
| sing | sang | sung |
| speak | spoke | spoken |
| steal | stole | stolen |
| swim | swam | swum |
| take | took | taken |
| wear | wore | worn |
| write | wrote | written |

# Songs

## LESSON 5 **Come along now**

Come along now
And meet your partners.
Move your desk and chairs.
Come along now
And greet your partners.
Move your desk and chairs.

Take a seat
And face your partners.
It's fun to work in pairs.
Ask for names
And ask for numbers.
It's fun to work in pairs.
It's fun to work in pairs.

Come along now
And meet your partners.
Move your desk and chairs.
Come along now
And greet your partners.
Move your desk and chairs.

Take a seat
And face your partners.
It's fun to work in pairs.
Ask more questions
Get more answers.
It's fun to work in pairs.
It's fun to work in pairs.

Come along now
And meet your partners.
Move your desk and chairs.
Come along now
And greet your partners.
Move your desk and chairs.

## LESSON 9 **Save the tiger**

Save the tiger.
Save the whale and the panda.
Save the tiger.
Save the whale and the gorilla.
Save the elephant in Africa
The eagle in America.
Save the wildlife of the world.
Save the tiger!

## LESSON 14 **People of today**

She's a woman of today
On the TV screen,
Selling frozen food
Or French icecream.
With her grey-green eyes
And shining hair
Her perfect teeth
And skin so fair
She's a perfect woman of today.
She's a perfect woman of today.

He's a man of today
In a magazine,
Selling aftershave
Or margarine.
He's got dark brown eyes
And a lovely tan
And the sort of looks
That make a man
Look handsome in a very modern way,
Look handsome in a very modern way.

She's a woman of today
On the TV screen,
Selling frozen food
Or French icecream.
He's a man of today
In a magazine
Selling aftershave
Or margarine.
They're perfect people of today.
They're perfect people of today.

## LESSON 30 **Funny family**

Oh, what a family.
What a funny family.
Oh, what a funny family!
We haven't any money
But we're really very funny.
And we're happy, just as happy as can be.
Happy, just as happy as can be.

My mother
Is a kung fu teacher.
They call her China tea.
My dad
Is a lighthouse keeper,
Out in the middle of the sea.
My granny's
In a cupboard in the garden.
Sister Susie
Wears a cabbage on her head.
Brother Charlie
Keeps his money in a bucket.
Uncle Harry
Keeps a python in his bed.

Oh, what a family.
What a funny family.
Oh, what a funny family!
We haven't any money
But we're really very funny.
And we're happy, just as happy as can be.
Happy, just as happy as can be.

**Longman Group UK Limited**
*Longman House, Burnt Mill, Harlow,*
*Essex CM20 2JE, England*
*and Associated Companies throughout the world.*

First published 1986
Twenty-second impression 1995

ISBN 0-582-51400-2

**Designed by** Nucleus design Associates
**Illustrated by** Chris Ryley,
with Michael Stafford , Julie Tennent, Andrew Aloof,
Tony Ross, Peter Dennis, Tony Kenyon

Set in Scantext Palatino
Printed in Italy by G. Canale & C. S.p.A. Borgaro T.se - Turin
GC/18

The publishers would like to point out that all characters in the
book are completely fictitious.

## Acknowledgements

**The authors and publishers would like to thank the**
**following for their invaluable comments on the manuscript:**
**Luciano Mariani, Serena Pasinetti, Eddie Edmundson,**
**Regina Guimaráes, Janet Dangar, Marisol Valcarcel,**
**Mercedes Verdú, Mercedes López de Blas, Ana Okamika,**
**Ana Fernandez, Antony Loproto.**

We are grateful to D C Thomson & Co Ltd for permission to reproduce an
adapted version of the article '24 hours with Anne McCrodden' from *Jackie*
magazine no 1074 (4/8/84).

We are grateful to the following for permission to reproduce copyright
photographs:

Ace Photo Agency/Paul Craven for page 20 (bottom left inset); All-Sport
Photographic Ltd for page 46 (top left) & 46 (bottom left); Art Directors Photo
Library for pages 13 (top middle) & 18 (right); Associated Sports
Photography for page 46 (top right); Bob Thomas Sports Photography for
page 46 (bottom right); British Tourist Authority for pages 53 (top left) & 71·
(left); Bruce Coleman Ltd for page 58 (middle right); Camera Press Ltd for
pages 6 (top middle) 13 (top right), 19 (bottom), 58 (top middle), 58 (middle
left), 58 (bottom left) & 58 (bottom right); The J. Allan Cash Photo Library for
pages 19 (bottom inset), 20 (top right inset) & 68 (top left); Colorific!/Mary
Ellen Mark/Visages for page 17 (right); Colorific!/B. Bartholomew for page
31; Daily Telegraph Colour Library for page 10 (middle); David Redfern
Photography for page 6 (bottom right); European Design Partnership for
page 57 (top); Geoff Morgan Photography for page 68 (top right); Image
Bank/Gerald Brimacombe for page 20 (bottom right inset); The John
Hillelson Agency Ltd/SYGMA for page 63 (top); Leo Mason Photo Library
for pages 17 (middle) & 46 (top middle); Licensiado Jose Agasto for page 23;
Longman Photographic Unit for pages 10 (bottom), 25-26, 65 & 67; Marion &
Tony Morrison South American Pictures for page 19 (top inset); Anders
Mathlein for page 55; Reproduced by permission of the National Postal
Museum for page 16 (top right); Photo Library International-Leeds for page
68 (bottom left); Pictor International-London for pages 13 (bottom middle) &
58 (top right); Pictorial Press Ltd for page 27 (middle right), 27 (bottom left) &
27 (bottom right); Picturepoint-London for pages 10 (top), 19 (top), 20 (top
left inset), 20 (top left), 20 (top right), 20 (bottom left), 20 (bottom right), 37,
53 (top middle), 53 (top right), 53 (bottom left), 57 (bottom) & 71 (right);
Graham Portlock for pages 65/66 (bottom); RETNA Pictures Ltd for page 27
(top left); Rex Features Ltd for pages 6 (bottom middle), 17 (left), 18 (upper
middle) & 18 (middle); Rogers & Cowan, Inc. for page 27 (top right); Chris
Ryley for page 57 (middle); Syndication International Library for page 18
(top) & 18 (left); By arrangement with D.C. Thomson & Co. Ltd. © D.C.
Thomson & Co. Ltd 1984 for page 79; Tim Graham Picture Library for page 6
(top left), 6 (top right) & 6 (bottom left); Tony Stone Photo Library-London
for page 13 (top left), 13 (bottom left), 13 (bottom right), 24, 53 (bottom right)
& 58 (top left); Topham Picture Library for pages 63 (bottom) & 68 (bottom
right); © 1984 Tritec Music Ltd. under licence to EMI Records/Francesco
Scavulla for page 27 (middle); Reprinted with the permission of Wimpy
International Limited for page 49 (right).